EARLY PRAISE FOR MARKETING FLEXOLOGY

"Kodak, Nokia, BlackBerry and many other famous brands have lost their luster because they were resistant to change. A dose of Marketing Flexology could have saved them."

Al Ries, author, Positioning: The Battle for Your Mind

"Whether you are marketing a brand, a company or yourself, Engelina Jaspers' insights are smart, informed and can be put to work right away. If you dare to succeed, put Marketing Flexology at the top of your books to read."

David Sable, Global CEO, Y&R

"Engelina Jaspers has written a must-read for marketers searching for strategies and an action plan to embrace and embolden change within their organizations and throughout their career . . . Read this book — and learn from one of the best."

Chris Curtin, Chief Brand Officer, Visa

"Engelina Jaspers redefines the role of marketing in today's customer-centric hyper-speed world. If you want to keep ahead of disruption, Marketing Flexology will show you how."

Vyomesh (VJ) Joshi, CEO and President, 3D Systems

"Every marketing leader must read this book! Engelina Jaspers explains why you need insight and agility to meet today's customer and business demands and lays out an incredibly practical and comprehensive four-step framework for how to get ahead. Packed with insights, tools, and tips that Engelina developed during her years leading marketing organizations, Marketing Flexology is the guidebook that will help you, your team, and your company navigate the current era of disruption and chaos and thrive."

Denise Lee Yohn, author of the bestselling books
What Great Brands Do and FUSION

MARKETING FLEXOLOGY

*How to Outsmart Change
and Future-proof Your Career*

Engelina Jaspers

FLEX PRO MEDIA

Marketing Flexology: *How to Outsmart Change and Future-proof Your Career*

Cover credit: JetLaunch
Book design credit: JetLaunch
Editor credit: Justin Spizman

BUS043000   BUSINESS & ECONOMICS / Marketing / General
BUS041000   BUSINESS & ECONOMICS / Management
BUS071000   BUSINESS & ECONOMICS / Leadership
BUS012000   BUSINESS & ECONOMICS / Careers / General

Printed in the United States of America.

First Printing: May 2018

978-1-7320154-0-1 (Hardcover)
978-1-7320154-1-8 (pbk)
978-1-7320154-2-5 (ebook)
978-1-7320154-3-2 (audiobook)

Library of Congress Control Number: 2018903494

DEDICATION

To Marshall, Graham, Vanessa, and Bryce: Never Stop Flexing.

TABLE OF CONTENTS

Flex or Die
ix

Chapter 1: Shift Happens
1

Chapter 2: Your CTA
12

Chapter 3: Speed to Insight
24

Chapter 4: Agility in Action
37

Chapter 5: The Marketing Shake(up)
52

Chapter 6: A Splash of Creativity
61

Chapter 7: Marketing Flexology Mindset
73

Chapter 8: Marketing Flexology Foundation
84

Chapter 9: Marketing Flexology Dials
100

Chapter 10: Marketing Flexology Tools
116

Chapter 11: Putting into Practice
135

Conclusion
143

Notes (Bibliography)
149

About the Author
163

One Last CTA
165

FLEX OR DIE

Survival is a powerful motivator. In fact, survival jolted my obsession for marketing agility. Over a thirty-year corporate career, I experienced more than my fair share of business upheaval and management change, accompanied by an equal number of marketing reinventions. While I was at the forefront leading the charge for some of these transformations, I was also on the receiving end and bearing the brunt of many others.

These experiences offered insight into what separated the career winners from the career losers. The winners—those who retained their budgets, their teams, their standing, and their jobs—were agile. In contrast, the losers were rigid and stuck in the status quo. Simply put, they couldn't adjust and fell victim to changing market conditions and company fluctuations.

In addition to being agile, the winners maintained steadfast roles, metrics, and lean teams, knew when to outsource, and managed flat and flexible budgets. The losers had just the opposite: bloated teams with roles designed around people versus needs, unclear accountability, soft metrics, and inflated runaway budgets.

I also uncovered a unique mindset that only the winners possessed. I call it a *business-first mindset,* and cultivating this trait is by far the most important thing a dynamic marketing leader can do. It goes like this: When faced with any business decision, place your company and customers first—before your team and before yourself. It may feel counterintuitive, but it works. All of these experiences led me to develop the *Marketing Flexology* management framework, a mindset and a toolset for future-proofing your career, your team, and your marketing platform. Whether you're building a new group, expanding an existing one, downsizing or transforming, the pages that follow will help you design a resilient marketing foundation that can withstand any business fluctuation, management change, or crisis *du jour*. The pace of business has accelerated over the past several years and shows no signs of slowing. It's time to take control before someone else does.

One way to take control is to dismiss some of marketing's commonly-held "truths" that are actually false. My all-time favorite false truism is "Marketing is part art and part science." In fact, a quick Google search of "is marketing art or science?" returns over 20 million articles, an indication of just how widespread this time-worn notion has become. The great debate over whether *art* or *science* is most crucial to the success of a marketing campaign has been raging for nearly a century. It has sparked many battles over budgets and resources, including today's tug-of-war between brand marketers focused on creating experiences and demand marketers devoted to funnel performance.

Frankly, the art versus science debate is as outdated as hotels without Wi-Fi. The seismic shifts of the past decade require a new marketing practice, one that embraces brand *and* demand and is steeped in real-time insight *and* speed to market. Those that have adjusted are thriving and growing. And as you can imagine, those still debating art versus science are being leapfrogged by today's modern marketer. Marketing agility means adjusting in the face of change, and being content with the status quo or "accepted" ways of doing things is a recipe for disaster.

Exerting the time and finding the patience for unreliable focus groups, drawn-out brand tracking studies, combative agency shootouts, and expensive management consultants have vanished. Companies need a 24/7 lifeline to real-time customer insight and a marketing capability to seize upon customer truths at a moment's notice.

Sure, creativity and analytics are still important, but they're no longer sufficient to capture today's eight-second-attention-span consumer. A new paradigm fixated on customer insight and speed to market is necessary.

Today's marketing is more like a cocktail. *It requires a mix of insight and agility—shaken well—and served with a splash of creativity.* I call this new elixir *Marketing Flexology.* No, I'm not advocating a return to the "Mad Men" era of the 1960s, known for big personalities, power, ego, sexism, and its three-martini lunches. I am, however, encouraging a renaissance of marketing's most fundamental role: understanding markets and consumers better than anyone else around.

In the chapters that follow, I show you step-by-step the mindset followed by the necessary tools to compete in today's better-faster-cheaper-smarter world.

In the first half of the book (Chapters 1 through 6), we examine the forces that transformed marketing from its origins as *art and science* to a modern-day practice requiring nothing short of *insight and agility.* This new paradigm requires an updated way of managing and leading today's marketing function, which we cover step-by-step in the second half of the book (Chapters 7 through 11).

In Chapter 1, we trace how both the customer and the marketing profession have transformed over the past sixty years of modern practice. I outline five key shifts that have redefined today's modern marketing practice, the most seismic of which has been a shift from *art and science* to *insight and agility.*

In Chapter 2, we look at the four motivations for organizational change, both natural and engineered, including examples of companies that have radically transformed their business. We also look at creating our own *call to action* to spur change.

In Chapter 3, we explore strategies to become an *insight machine* and accelerate customer decision making. The need to quickly move from customer insight to customer experience has never been greater, nor the challenge more daunting.

We turn our newfound *listening and learning* into high-speed *execution and iteration* in Chapter 4. We cover the three main pillars of marketing agility: *organizational agility*, *personal agility*, and *learning agility*.

Chapter 5 looks at the inevitable marketing shakeup, which has become a hallmark for our profession, and how to prepare your team for the next crisis *du jour*.

In Chapter 6, we add the *splash of creativity* to our *Marketing Flexology* elixir. In an age where data, technology, and analytics have overrun the creative process, we look at how to sharpen our creativity and break through the dwindling supply of consumer attention.

In Chapter 7, we look at the most important traits of a dynamic marketing leader, beginning with adopting a *business-first mindset*.

We then turn to the underlying *Marketing Flexology* foundation in Chapter 8—*purpose*, *people*, and *process*. We delve into three main charters for a marketing organization, successful people strategies that work, and the six core marketing processes all leaders must have in place.

Chapter 9 considers the four things in a marketer's arsenal that are 100 percent within our control. How we fine-tune these dials—*people*, *programs*, *budgets*, and *agencies*—often determines how seamlessly we can react to unplanned change and prevent a career blowout.

In Chapter 10, we explore five core strategic marketing tools every marketing leader needs in their management toolbox to maximize their team's effectiveness. We look at what they are, why they're important, and what each contains in detail.

We put it all into practice in the final chapter, Chapter 11, with a ninety-day challenge and a week-by-week action plan to transition to a *Marketing Flexology* mindset and toolset.

Each of these chapters will help you and your business become more agile and focused. As times change, and the marketing industry continues to reinvent itself, we have to respond to the turning tides. If not, we'll be left behind, extinct, and laid to rest in the marketing graveyard. Remember EF Hutton, TWA, and General Foods? How about Borders, Circuit City, and Enron? These brands were once household names, but not anymore. Together, we can ensure we are taking the bold route, leading the charge, and setting an example for the rest of our industry. Let's get started, shall we?

Chapter 1

SHIFT HAPPENS

"Things which don't shift and grow are dead things."
—Leslie Marmon Silko

Marketing has been around for as long as humans have had something to sell. As a business practice, though, marketing is a relatively new discipline. Marketing departments within companies first sprung up in the middle of the twentieth century. All you needed was a good product prior to the 1960s—be it coffee, tea, or whiskey. That all changed with the advent of mass production and a corresponding rise in competition and commoditization. Marketing flourished when companies suddenly could no longer easily sell everything made possible by mass production.

Advancements in technology and transportation further crowded markets and pushed businesses to remain competitive by hiring marketers and creating marketing divisions. The ranks of professional marketers have swelled ever since, reaching 10.6 million worldwide, as measured by the number of LinkedIn members who list "marketing" or "marketer" in their job titles. Most every aspect of our profession has changed over the past sixty years of marketing practice—not only *what* we do as marketers and *how* we do it, but also the actual *value* marketing provides.

As times have changed, so has the approach to marketing. This has led to quite possibly the largest shift by far, which forms the overall premise of this book—that the view of marketing as merely a combination of art and science is no longer sufficient in today's customer centric hyper speed world. While creative and analytics still inform our marketing practices, they have been superseded by the need for real-time customer insight and speed to market. Frankly, customers don't care about what blend of art and science goes into our marketing strategies and programs. They only care about how well our messages hit a nerve and fulfill a need.

In my thirty-plus years of marketing practice, I have seen the marked polarization between marketing *artists* and marketing *scientists*. Our customers and their buying journeys are much more complicated today, and a simple either-or, yes-or-no solution doesn't work. The better answer today is "It depends." I have also witnessed a new breed of marketing professionals who have successfully bridged art and science. These are marketing creatives whose artistic sensibilities were largely informed by analytics, as well as marketing analysts itching for a way to express their findings as stories. In the chapters that follow, I share with you the mindset and the toolset needed to excel in today's new art and science: *Marketing Flexology.*

In addition to the seismic shift from *art and science* to *insight and agility*, other significant marketing transformations have occurred over the past many decades. These include a change in customer expectations, the role of the chief marketing officer (CMO), the marketing mix, and brand ownership. There are certainly others, including just about every marketing tactic and delivery channel imaginable, but these changes are a good place to start our conversation. Stepping back and examining these shifts reminds us not to become too comfortable with our current tactics, favorite marketing programs, or preferred communication style. As the landscape changes, and it will, marketing agility must be our watchword. To that end, let's review each of these transformational shifts.

Shift 1: Beyond Art and Science

If you haven't already searched the phrase "Is marketing art or science?" then do it now. You'll get over 20 million search results, an indication of just how pervasive this paradigm and debate has become in our lexicon and in our thinking. Many continue to believe marketing falls predominantly into one of two categories:

(1) Creative and artistic sensibilities (art) or

(2) Analysis and measurement (science)

These two proponents then endlessly debate whether creative or analytics is most crucial to the success of a marketing campaign, all the while jousting over budget, resources, and authority.

James W. Culliton, professor of marketing at Harvard University, had a better mental model describing marketers as "mixers of ingredients." Dr. Culliton used the colorful metaphor in his 1948 article "The Management of Marketing Costs," which later led to the development of "the marketing mix" and 4Ps, which I talk about in Shift 4.

Dr. Culliton went on to explain that sometimes a marketing executive "follows a recipe prepared by others, sometimes prepares his own recipe as he goes along, sometimes adapts a recipe to the ingredients immediately available, and sometimes experiments with or develops ingredients no one else has yet tried."

His analogy was insightful, clairvoyant, and applicable to how marketing is practiced today. It's the new art and science I call *Marketing Flexology*. The essential *mix* required to outsmart change and to future-proof your career is this: Combine equal parts insight and agility, shake well, and serve with a splash of creativity.

Shift 2: Evolving Customer Expectations

I remember it as if only yesterday. I was a marketing newbie, just starting my career at the Eastman Kodak Company. Kodak, at that time, was a big-league player and a household name. They ranked among the top twenty of the Fortune 500. At their peak, they commanded 90 percent of all film sales and 85 percent of all camera sales in the US. They also ranked as the fourth most valuable brand in the world.

A sign that hung outside the office of our vice president of corporate communications said: "Good, fast or cheap. Pick two." As an ambitious twentysomething, I took the adage to heart.

If you wanted high quality fast, it was going to cost you. If you wanted high quality at a low cost, you had to expect a long delivery time. If you wanted speedy delivery at the lowest price, you couldn't expect high quality. And you never, ever got all three.

To a marketer, the good-fast-cheap conundrum was gospel (and a pretty darn good defense). Our craft was always a tradeoff of budget, deadline, and quality.

Fast-forward thirty years. Today that paradigm is laughable. It is no longer acceptable to deliver subpar quality over a protracted time horizon or at an excessive price. We need to be better, faster, cheaper, and smarter, all at the same time. The new adage is: "Better, faster, cheaper, smarter. Deliver all."

Customers are demanding a new level of service and engagement and rewarding businesses that deliver all. These ever-evolving customer expectations are now the second shift in the marketing industry.

Shift 3: Changing Role of the Chief Marketing Office (CMO)

While some would argue that marketing fundamentals remain unchanged, no one can dispute that marketing strategies, delivery mechanisms, and even the way in which we apply creativity have dramatically changed over the decades.

Not surprisingly, the changing role of the CMO tracks with technology advances that ushered in new mediums through which to communicate a message. With the mainstream adoption of radio and television, marketing heads were largely creative directors and broadcast advertisers. The emergence of desktop publishing and the personal computer led to an explosion in design and print advertisers.

With the advent of the Internet and email, marketing's role expanded to include online marketing, pitting leading-edge *e-marketers* against diehard print, billboard, and broadcast advertisers.

Mobile technology, specifically 2G mobile network advancements, paved the way for increased cell phone usage. Taking that one step further, emerging mediums like SMS (text) messaging became new marketing mediums. What followed in rapid succession were search marketing, SEO, blogging, social media, ecommerce, online video . . . all at a dizzying pace for marketers to keep up with. With each of these advances, large areas of responsibilities were added to the CMO's bailiwick.

In just the past several years, we have seen a huge expansion of the CMO role. Research and consulting firm Gartner found that in more than 30 percent of all organizations, at least some aspects of sales, IT, and customer experience now report to the CMO.[1]

Some are suggesting new marketing titles, including chief marketing technologist—part strategist, part creative director, part technology leader, and part teacher.[2] Others argue that CMOs must take control of the customer experience and take on customer service as part of their remit.[3] And CMOs are the most likely of the C-suite, and nearly twice as likely as CIOs, to lead digital transformation efforts within their organization, research shows.[4] Some companies are eliminating the CMO role completely, in hopes of accelerating growth and agility. In 2018, Hyatt Hotels Corporation nixed its global CMO position, merging its guest and customer engagement function with marketing under a new chief commercial officer role. Coca-Cola took a route similar to Hyatt's when in 2017 it eliminated its global CMO role, creating instead the role of chief growth officer.[5]

Chief digital officer, chief customer officer, chief experience officer, chief marketing technologist, chief growth officer . . . no, all these titles are not an indictment of a marketing identity crisis. Rather, they are a realization by the executive ranks of the pivotal role marketing can play in growth and customer satisfaction. Is it any surprise, then, that executive search firm Russell Reynolds finds CMOs the most innovative and adaptive members of the C-suite?[6] We have to be.

Shift 4: Remixing the Marketing Mix

E. Jerome McCarthy, an academic and author, proposed the concept of the 4Ps marketing mix in his 1960 book, *Basic Marketing: A Managerial Approach.*[7] The textbook's nineteenth edition was published in 2013 and continues to be one of the top textbooks used in university marketing education. Little wonder the 4Ps are firmly imprinted in our marketing psyches. Case in point: In a 2017 *Marketing Week* poll, 77 percent of marketers answered "yes" when asked if the 4Ps of marketing were relevant to their jobs today.[8]

The 4Ps—often referred to as the marketing mix—provided a simple way to capture the controllable variables required to market a product or service: *product, price, place,* and *promotion. Product* refers to a good or service being offered by a company. *Price* is the cost consumers pay for a product. *Place* is how the product is distributed and where it is sold. *Promotion* is made up of the elements chosen to promote the product or service and includes advertising, public relations, and promotional strategies and tactics.

A much more relevant model, which you don't hear much about, is the 4Cs. Robert F. Lauterborn, International Paper and GE marketing executive turned professor, proposed this marketing paradigm in 1990.

Lauterborn suggested replacing the prevailing "inside-out" perspective where a company's products sit squarely in the middle of the marketing mindset, with an "outside-in" strategy that views customer value as its starting and end point. Author Seth Godin said it well: "You don't find customers for your products. You find products for your customers."

In the 4Cs model *product* has been replaced by *customer needs.* Instead of focusing on the features, advantages, and benefits of your product, the focus is on your customers' needs, wants, and desires.

Price in the 4Cs model has been replaced by *cost to satisfy* that need, want, and desire. This revised thinking realizes it is no longer just about the price but, rather, a myriad of value judgments and tradeoffs that accompany any decision purchase (psychological, political, economic, and social good). This can take many forms, including the packaging, the out-of-box experience, the ease of operating, the sense of pride, accomplishment, or esteem, and the belief that your purchase is giving something back to a worthy cause or the environment.

Place has been replaced by *convenience to buy*. Consumers now decide how and when to buy your product or service through a direct sales representative, brick-and-mortar retail store, flexible online shopping options, intermediaries or third-parties, or even through vending machines.

The final C in the 4C model is *communication*. It replaces *promotion* and recognizes that today's marketing is an engaging, integrated, and continual dialogue with a customer.

FROM THE 4Ps TO THE 4Cs

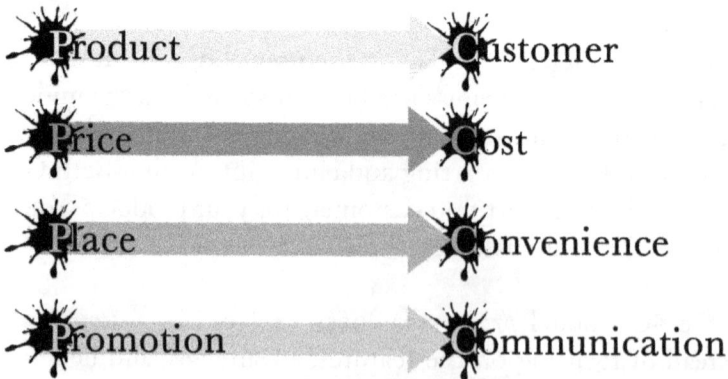

Product → Customer

Price → Cost

Place → Convenience

Promotion → Communication

Shift 5: Shift in Brand Ownership

There was a time, and a very grand time it was, when companies owned their brands. That is no longer the case. The final shift we will discuss relates to brand ownership.

In a different era, marketing leaders would decide what message to send, to which audience, through which media, at what time, and with which frequency. It was an era of big brands, mass marketing, mass media, and carefully orchestrated *push* brand messages.

Social media changed all that. As Scott Cook, cofounder of Intuit says, "A brand is no longer what we tell the consumer. It is what consumers tell each other." Today, every employee, every past-present-future customer, every advocate, dissenter, and stakeholder lends their voice to a brand's cacophony.

With an angry tweet, a Facebook "like," or a YouTube satirical spoof on a company's advertising (think MasterCard's *Priceless* campaign), consumers are bringing brand experiences to light. Even Yelp reviews in New York City are helping city health authorities find restaurants that aren't up to snuff from a cleanliness, safety, or food preparation perspective.[9]

Jill Avery, a senior lecturer at Harvard Business School, describes the power shift from marketers to consumers as "open source branding," where consumers not only discuss and disseminate branded content, they also create it.

Given this paradigm shift, you might ask, "Is brand management still important?" It's more important than ever. While traditional advertising is having less effect on buying habits, consumers today are making conscious statements with their purchases. Brands serve as a form of shorthand that helps consumers define and showcase to the world who they are and what they value. Despite an increased aversion to advertising, studies show that millennials are more brand loyal than any other generation, with just over one-half of them saying they are extremely loyal or quite loyal to their favorite brands.[10]

So while brand leaders no longer fully control the perception of their companies and products, they do control how well they meet their customers' engagement expectations.[11] Today's smart brand leaders are exploring new ways to unleash and synchronize brand messages and voices across every touch point in the customer journey.

Summary

Marketing is an ever-changing landscape as are consumers. Consumers are no longer as homogenous as they once were in the baby boomer era. We now have new generations of consumers to understand and with whom to engage, including millennials, Generation X, Y, Z, and beyond. We need to continually challenge, adjust, and advance our marketing strategies, our teams, and ourselves to stay ahead.

The five shifts outlined in this chapter represent the substantial changes over the past sixty years. But more are coming. The future is exciting and bright, yet filled with the urgency to reinvent and transform.

Many of the marketing paradigms created by our analog ancestors will continue to be challenged, updated, and replaced—as they should. Our world, our markets, and our customers are in constant evolution. Our marketing practices need to keep pace. Adopting a *Marketing Flexology* framework is your best career insurance.

Chapter 1 Key Takeaways:

- While marketing is a relatively new business discipline, it has undergone significant transformation over the past sixty years.

- During this time, there have been significant marketing shifts, the most seismic of which has been the shift from *art and science* to *insight and agility*.

- Five shifts have redefined today's modern marketing practice: (1) beyond art and science, (2) evolving customer expectations, (3) the changing role of the CMO, (4) a remix of the marketing mix and 4Ps, and (5) the shift in brand ownership from companies to consumers.

- Marketing is a continually evolving profession; transformation is the new normal.

- Marketing agility is a prerequisite for success and your best career protection.

Chapter 2

YOUR CTA

"There lives in each of us a hero awaiting the call to action."
—*H. Jackson Brown Jr.*

We marketers know a thing or two about CTAs. We use them in just about every campaign we create.

CTAs—calls to action—are a prompt (in the form of a phrase or button) that induces a reader, listener, or viewer to perform a specific act. The best CTAs offer the target audience a valuable benefit in exchange for taking that next step, provide clear direction, and create a sense of urgency. Here are some popular examples you've probably heard before:

Call now for your free quote!
Subscribe today to get more valuable tips!
Click here to download free templates!
Get your advance copy before it goes public!
Start my free no-obligation trial!
Sign up and reserve your spot today!
Don't delay, get your free evaluation now!

CTAs are littered across our marketing materials and for good reason: They successfully get people to act *now*.

While most marketing CTAs are *engineered* to create a desired change, they occur naturally and frequently in the business world, which we'll look at next.

Organizational Change

In business, a change in model, a change in market, a change in management, or a change in metrics often trigger CTAs. I refer to these as the 4Ms—the 4 motivations for organizational change. Let's unpack each one in greater detail.

The First Motivation: Change in Model

Sometimes, changing your business model is the only way for a company to survive. It could be as part of a company's natural evolution from startup to IPO to maturity. It could be as an outcome of an acquisition, merger, or divestiture. Or it could be a conscious decision to shift away from your flagship products as the following four companies did.

IBM is one of the rare companies to have thrived over a century after it was founded by continually evolving its core product offerings. The company first sold commercial scales and punch card tabulators, and, later, massive mainframe computers and calculators. Today, IBM is focused on software, consulting, and IT services.[1]

DuPont shares a similar story. In 1802, Lammot du Pont developed a less expensive way to manufacture black gunpowder, which also produced a stronger blast. Today, DuPont sells polymer adhesives, insecticides, fire extinguishers, and weatherization systems, a far cry from its original model.

NCR also successfully reinvented its core offering. Founded in 1884 as the National Cash Register Company and maker of the first mechanical cash registers, the company changed its name to NCR Corporation in 1974 to symbolize its more diverse product lines, including bar code scanners and computers. Today, NCR calls itself a leader in omni-channel solutions.[2]

Formerly known as Flextronics, the company had evolved from a contract manufacturer to an electronics manufacturing company to an end-to-end supply-chain solutions company. But the company's reputation as one of the world's largest electronics manufacturers still remained. Enter Michael Mendenhall, the company's first chief marketing and chief communications officer. In 2015, Mendenhall led not only a name change from Flextronics to Flex, but also a strategic repositioning for the company. Six months following the rebrand, the company's share value had increased 44 percent, much of which could be attributed to the company's new narrative and communications.[3]

In the past, many brands lived to be 100 years old. Today, the average life span of companies in the S&P 500 is fifteen years.[4] Just as companies can increase their odds of survival by evolving their business models, marketers, too, must continually evolve their model and practice. That is the basis of the first motivation for organizational change.

The Second Motivation: Change in Market

Transformations are often sparked by a fluctuation in market conditions. A competitive advance, entry of a new market player, market consolidation, and a technology disruption can each necessitate an organizational change. But perhaps the biggest market driver is appealing to a new audience or generation of customers.

In 2006, Old Spice was a seventy-year-old brand, predominately associated with old men and losing ground.[5] But it became a cultural phenomenon and overnight success after a now-legendary advertising, social media, and video campaign. Sales were up 125 percent year over year by the end of July 2010, and Old Spice had become the #1 selling body wash brand for men in the United States.

KFC has had similar success appealing to a new generation of consumers while also rekindling nostalgia in an older generation.

The company has embarked on a multiyear revitalization strategy, which includes not only a new Colonel and less messy menu items for a generation that wants to eat something on the go, but also a return to its Southern hospitality roots. Part of the plan is to appeal to older adults who no longer frequent the chain but have fond memories of KFC before it became associated with fast food.

These are just a few examples of the success stories. Sadly, other brands have not been as successful in appealing to new markets or new generations of consumers.[6]

The Snapple brand of tea and juice drinks has gone through many changes since the company originated in Long Island, New York, in 1972. Snapple found its success using quirky, irreverent, and fun advertising, and a niche distribution strategy, typically selling one bottle at a time in convenience stores. When Quaker Oats acquired the brand in 1994, it quickly set out to bring Snapple to every grocery store and chain restaurant possible. The company's efforts failed miserably. Quaker completely missed the Snapple audience and appeal, and after just twenty-seven months sold it at the fire-sale price of $300 million—$1.4 billion less than it paid for the company.

Another sad example is Sears. Once the stalwart department store for working-class American families, the more than 130-year-old brand is now perceived as out of step and out of style. Toward the beginning of 2000, Sears found itself struggling to remain profitable and relevant amidst the successes of big-box stores like Target and Walmart. A hedge-fund investor whose fund controlled Kmart decided to merge the two companies, and in 2005 they became Sears Holdings. It seemed to be a promising merger, but it hasn't stopped the downward spiral of the two brands. According to the company's website, Sears and Kmart continue to close unprofitable stores and hold liquidation sales, as the company "transforms our business model so that our physical store footprint and our digital capabilities match the needs and preferences of our members."

Remember, it's not only about successfully marketing to millennials, but also about anticipating and being prepared for what's next in an ever-changing marketplace.

The Third Motivation: Change in Management

A management change can also prompt a CTA, especially if the new chief is brought in from the outside. It's often a signal that the company has lost its way, needs to grow in a new direction, or requires a reset. Turnover at the top almost always sparks upheaval. But it could also lead to opportunity. Here are a few examples that highlight this point:

The arrival in July 2006 of new CEO Angela Ahrendts turned Burberry from an aging British icon into a global luxury brand. When over sixty managers flew in from around the world into classic damp British weather for a strategy session, not one was wearing a Burberry trench coat. "If our top people weren't buying our products, despite the great discount they could get, how could we expect customers to pay full price for them?" asked Ahrendts, who now runs Apple's retail division.[7] It was a sign of the challenges the company faced, including a meager two percent annual growth rate. Through refocus and a tightened rein on out-of-control licensing, by the end of fiscal year 2012, Burberry's revenues and operating income had doubled over the previous five years.

When Jorgen Vig Knudstorp came in as Lego CEO in 2004, the Danish toymaker was on the brink of bankruptcy. Knudstorp, a former McKinsey consultant, launched a painful turnaround plan. He laid off nearly half of the firm's employees as he dramatically consolidated and streamlined operations and components. Knudstorp also began personally engaging with customers in their homes and at fan events to bring creativity and simplicity back to the company.[8] By 2013, Lego was the world's most profitable toymaker.

Both of these examples highlight how hard it can be for an existing team to take action when their company has clearly drifted off course. Sometimes it takes a new leader, with a fresh set of eyes and a change mandate, to right the course.

Most always, a change in management leads to a re-examination and a change for the marketing organization. If you've built an agile marketing team, being able to pivot at a moment's notice might be your opportunity to shine.

The Fourth Motivation: Change in Metrics

The fourth trigger for marketing reinventions is misaligned metrics resulting from a new direction. As a marketing leader, you may be focused on brand awareness, marketing effectiveness, and customer experience, and have built your team and allocated budgets accordingly. Based on shifting priorities, senior management may now expect marketing to drive incremental revenue, share of wallet, and customer advocacy. This usually requires a reset of marketing programs and a redistribution of people and budgets.

Put yourself in the heels of the CMO in each of the following examples, and then consider how well you and your team would be able to respond.

In 2012, Procter & Gamble chairman and CEO Bob McDonald told analysts in an earnings call that the company was looking to lower promotion costs, which had historically run 9 to 11 percent of revenue. With earnings softening and under fire for its bloated promotion budget, the company was turning to social media to improve its return on investment. In 2015, P&G announced a multiyear agency consolidation initiative expected to save $500 million annually in agency fees and production costs, incremental to what the company had already accomplished through belt-tightening efforts of recent years. The agency consolidation continues today.[9]

McGraw-Hill Education (MHE) is one of the big three educational publishers. In 2014, David Levin was brought in as president and CEO to transition the company from a traditional textbook publisher to a provider of digital content and technology-enabled learning solutions. Traditional textbook publishing is not known for spending heavily on marketing, and MHE's long-tenured execs were reluctant to invest in rebranding. Tough tradeoffs were needed. Previously, a large portion of the promotional budget was earmarked to provide complimentary copies of its printed books. By converting to e-sampling of books, the marketing team was able to carve out needed monies for new content, talent, processes, and technology to help scale e-learning at a global level.[10]

Founded in 1918 as United Newspapers, UBM today is a multinational media company primarily focused on business-to-business (B2B) events. Over the years, the company has repositioned its focus to live events and online communities and away from its legacy printed magazines. Through more than 100 acquisitions and more than a dozen divestitures, UBM has reoriented the company from a broad media conglomerate focused in the UK and the US, into an events and communications business with a significant proportion of its business in emerging markets.

In each of these scenarios, change created an urgent call to action and, likely, a lot of turmoil across the marketing ranks. Change required new marketing skills and processes for UBM and McGraw-Hill Education as they digitally enabled their business models. Change led to fewer agencies and programs as P&G consolidated its agency roster and moved programs and budgets to social media. Only the most flexible and adaptive marketing organizations could survive these transformations and emerge unscathed.

In Chapter 8, we'll take a closer look at the marketing dials that form the foundation of *Marketing Flexology*. These include:

1. People

2. Programs

3. Budgets

4. Agencies

These are the only four dials to which marketing leaders can turn to achieve business and marketing objectives. Our ability to structure and manage these dials often determines how smoothly and successfully we can adjust to organizational change.

The unspoken truth is that there will always be a change in model, market, management, or metrics. It's the new reality in today's hypercompetitive fast-moving world. We had better get used to it and prepare ourselves to stay one step ahead of the transformation curve. Don't waste a good crisis by being unprepared.

Personal Change

Each of the motivations referenced in this chapter have at least one thing in common: They all involve a response to change. For many people, change is an unwelcome source of stress, anxiety, and fear. That's particularly true when change is thrust on us and we're not in control. But not all change is bad or unwanted, as Tim Kastelle, a student and teacher of innovation, reminds us.[11] Kastelle says, 'It turns out that people don't hate change at all. In many cases we actively seek out change. We move to a new city or country, we get married, we have children, we take a new job. These aren't just changes—these are massive changes. And we often seek them out. People don't resist change. At least, they don't when they expect the change to make their lives better.'

That's really the key, isn't it? If we are in control of the change and believe it will make our lives better, we're in. If not, we resist.

Create Your Own CTA

How, then, do we engineer change within our teams and our own careers, rather than merely reacting and responding to change? Here's where our skill in developing customer CTAs comes in handy. Earlier, I stated that strong CTAs have three things in common. They:

(1) Offer a valuable benefit

(2) Give clear direction

(3) Convey a sense of urgency

Let's apply these same three elements to create our own personal CTA.

Offer a Valuable Benefit

From my experience, the communicated goals of most change initiatives are either overly lofty, uninspiring, or nebulous. While companies may aim to restore #1 market leadership (lofty), reverse a downward sales trend (uninspiring), or increase the speed of innovation (nebulous), at the employee level they often fail to translate into tangible benefits.

As a result, employees frequently wonder *What do you want me to do with this?*, or *What should I be doing differently?*, or worse, *Why is this my problem?*

Successful CTAs answer the question *What's in it for me?* They inspire, motivate, encourage, and compel employees to own the problem, achieve the goal, and act in a way that benefits the company, and them, personally.

Successful CTAs provide a benefit in exchange for taking the requested action. If you take this action, we can avoid laying off employees. If you take this action, we all will receive a year-end bonus. If you take this action, we can fund the annual holiday party. Make it personal, make it valuable, and make it tangible.

Give Clear Direction

The second element of a successful CTA is providing clear direction. Most companies have dozens of change initiatives and business improvements that need attention—and usually all at the same time. We learned from customer CTAs that limiting the number of options actually increases the likelihood of success. Be clear about what you need your team, or yourself, to do and in what order of priority.

Successful CTAs use verbs to persuade. They aren't the *sign-up, register, subscribe,* or *call* verbs used in customer CTAs. Rather, they use specific actionable statements such as *stop doing X,* and *start doing Y&Z.*

Limiting the number of options and using direct, simple, and actionable language helps us give clear direction in our CTAs.

Convey a Sense of Urgency

The third common element of a CTA is creating a sense of urgency or scarcity. Deadlines and time limits make people act quickly rather than think too much, wait too long, or simply not respond. To create a sense of urgency, use urgent language in your CTA such as *now, immediately, today, hurry,* and *fast.*

Scarcity also works to convey a sense of urgency. When people know there are a limited number of days, seats, free tickets, job openings, or other enticing opportunities, they are propelled to action. Another powerful motivational tool is the fear of missing out (or FOMO). It's that anxious feeling of envy and insecurity that something more exciting is happening elsewhere and you're not included. (In fact, "FOMO" was officially added to the Oxford Dictionary in 2013.)

In the marketing world, a campaign, advertisement, or promotion without a call to action is considered incomplete and ineffective. The same holds true for any change initiative. To be effective, all change needs to provide your team with a valuable benefit in exchange for taking that next step, giving clear direction, and conveying a sense of urgency.

Will You Take the Next Step?

#IfIOnlyKnew is a trending hashtag on Twitter. It talks to interview techniques, dealing with your boss and coworkers, leadership skills, emotional intelligence, and a host of other career topics. There is no shortage of good advice or good intentions. However, there is a lack of action. I'd like to see a subsequent trending hashtag: #WhatWillYouDoNowThatYouKnow. Taking that next step is the hardest.

Seth Godin captured the sentiment well: "The easiest thing to do is react. The second easiest thing is to respond. But the hardest thing is to initiate. Initiating is difficult but that's what leaders do." Maybe we're hoping for better times, better luck, and better days ahead. Maybe we're just too busy to initiate a needed change. Maybe we're ignoring the warning signs of a subpar organization because we have too much invested in its success. Or, just maybe, we're waiting for that call to action. If so, here are a few of my favorites:

Transform or be transformed; the choice is yours.
Create your own "call to action."
There is no opportunity in comfort.
Change the rules before someone else does.
Don't waste a good crisis by being unprepared.

Summary

We've all heard why people are resistant to change: fear of failure, uncertainty, risk, loss of power or control, stepping outside one's comfort zone, and even inertia. Change requires effort—added time, skills, and learning—and that's why people often chose to stay right where they are. They subscribe to the *change only when you have to* mantra.

Whether we love change or hate it, we have no choice but to embrace it. To be sure, we will be faced with evermore-frequent organizational change in the years ahead, accompanied by an abundance of marketing course corrections. Perfecting our response to change, as well as initiating our own personal CTAs, will determine our career success or failure.

Chapter 2 Key Takeaways:

- Four motivations spur organizations to act: a change in model, market, management, or metrics (the 4Ms).

- Every organizational change creates a corresponding call to action (CTA).

- Just like companies, marketers must continually evolve their model and practice or face the consequences.

- Building a dynamic marketing organization that can pivot with business change can turn upheaval into opportunity.

- Strong customer CTAs have three things in common: They offer a valuable benefit, give clear direction, and convey a sense of urgency. Successful marketers apply these same three elements to create their *own* CTA.

Chapter 3

SPEED TO INSIGHT

"The best vision is insight."
—Malcolm S. Forbes

There has been a significant transformation in marketing practice over the past six decades, the most notable of which has been the shift from *art and science* to *insight and agility*. The need for high-speed listening, learning, execution, and iteration have leapfrogged creative (art) and data analytics (science). Insight and agility have become the new marketing art and science.

The legendary Jack Welch, former CEO of General Electric, recognized this when he said, "We have only two sources of competitive advantage: the ability to learn more about our customer faster than the competition, and the ability to turn that learning into action faster than the competition."

Here's where small businesses, entrepreneurs, and consultants have an edge: They interact with a handful of customers, listen to their input and feedback, and make improvements to their offerings, service, and operations in real time. That's *listening, learning, execution*, and *iteration* in action.

As businesses grow in size and complexity, they tend to develop natural silos where customer insights can become trapped. Each team collects the information they need for their function, their geography, or their business. That data is not easily or routinely shared across the enterprise. Getting at the trapped insights is often why companywide *voice of the customer* (VoC) programs get started.

After VoC programs reach a certain level of maturity, companies begin mapping their customer insights along a predictable journey: from awareness to consideration to preference to purchase to loyalty. The hope is that they can move prospects through the cycle quicker. Of course, the buyer's journey today is neither linear nor predictable. In fact, it's more like a bowl of spaghetti.[1] And, the customer gets to decide whether they use a fork, spoon, both, or neither.

The need to quickly move from customer insight to customer experience has never been greater, nor the challenge more daunting. In fact, it's one of the key arguments for adding CMOs to company boards. It can be invaluable to have someone with a strong pulse on the customer as major decisions are being discussed and made. Yet marketing-experienced executives are rarely invited to join a company's board of directors; only sixty-eight of the 9,800 board seats at Fortune 1000 companies are occupied by marketers.[2]

cAN yOu hEaR mE?

Customer insight can come from multiple sources and take many forms. These include: comments, complaints, unsolicited feedback, observation, market research, advisory boards, surveys, interviews, polling, tastings, online reviews, social media, shopping behavior, buying patterns, customer service interactions, and more. There is no shortage of data or customer insights.

Traditionally, companies have relied on a combination of quantitative data from surveys (such as for brand tracking and customer satisfaction) and qualitative insights from focus groups, interviews, and advisory boards.

There has been much debate over the effectiveness of these methods as they rely on a customer's memory and good intentions rather than on actual behavior. The focus group, in particular, has been chided and even proclaimed dead by *The Wall Street*

Journal.[3] They cite examples of failed business decisions made as a result of focus groups, including the famous replacement of Coca-Cola with a New Coke formula, which consumers widely rejected.

Focus group proponents, on the other hand, point to success stories such as the focus group that helped turn things around for Domino's Pizza. Based on feedback, Domino's improved its product, marketing, and results. Domino's promoted its turn-around in a 360-degree promotional campaign with the tagline "Oh Yes We Did." It worked. They enjoyed five straight years of positive same-store sales growth, which made Domino's among the fastest growing major quick-service restaurants along with Starbucks.[4]

In their book *Bottom-up Marketing*, even the legendary Al Ries and Jack Trout provide a cautionary reminder on market research. "There's nothing wrong with market research as long as you remember that marketing is a game of the future. Most market research is a report on the past." In his best-selling book *Blink*, Malcolm Gladwell makes a similar claim by stating market research is often wrong, particularly when assessing ideas that are new and different with consumers.

The prevailing consensus is that technology-driven tools do a better job in explaining consumer behavior than surveys and climate-controlled rooms with one-way mirrors. Not only are these new technology tools less expensive and less time-consuming to prepare and administer, they also increase *speed to insight*, which leads to real-time decision making and *speed to activation*.

Eric Reynolds, CMO of The Clorox Company, explains, "In the past, we might have run a TV campaign for 47 weeks and then we waited for 26 weeks to get the data back, analyze it and decide whether it's a good campaign or not. By then the entire year has gone by, which is not good." Clorox is aggressively transforming its approach, internal model, and agency lineup to become digital first, allowing the company to be more adaptive and responsive.[5] The move also includes new digital tools that can help the middle ranks improve decision making in less time.

Insights in Real Time

Many companies have turned to social media as a listening and learning tool. Social media conversations happen in your industry every minute of the day. While some companies choose to merely monitor these conversations by putting them into fancy dashboards for management to review, the more progressive companies jump into social media conversations with both feet. They realize it is a valuable opportunity to engage with customers in a meaningful dialogue, as Tesla Inc. and SpaceX CEO Elon Musk does.

When a Tesla owner tweeted the CEO complaining about fellow consumers hogging spots at a local charging station, Musk replied: "You're right, this is becoming an issue. Supercharge spots are meant for charging, not parking. Will take action." Six days later, Tesla announced a new policy and fleet-wide idle fee aimed at increasing Supercharge availability. The company's app alerts drivers when their car's charge is nearly complete and gives them a grace period of five minutes before the idle fee kicks in.[6]

One of the traps marketers fall into is believing that social data from platforms such as Facebook, Instagram, and Snapchat are only useful for social media marketing initiatives. These insights are relevant beyond social media marketing and should be shared and applied widely across the organization.

Online Brand Communities

Beyond social media, online brand communities, message boards, and review platforms offer another good venue for listening and learning. These forums are an insight-rich source of customer feedback on everything from existing products to new products, from service to support, from user complaints to compliments.

Social media strategist Megan Adams identifies five types of online communities:

(1) Interest: people who share the same interest or passion

(2) Action: communities of people trying to bring about change

(3) Place: groups linked by geography, such as cities, schools, and neighborhoods

(4) Practice: those who share the same profession or share a passion for the same activities

(5) Circumstance: people brought together by external events or situations[7]

By enabling co-creation and tapping into the collective intelligence of your customers, online communities are a great way to build trust, advocacy, and loyalty. They provide a platform for companies to test new ideas, develop new products, track customer service trends, gauge customer interest, and spot trends. Online communities also provide excellent case studies that you can use in your marketing activity (with permission, of course). Some of the best online brand communities include:[8]

- **Lugnet (Lego)**—where enthusiasts can find and submit ideas for new designs and even compete to become one of the brand's official next sets, with the creator receiving a percentage of final sales

- **Figment (Random House)**—a community of over 300,000 aspiring young adult writers who love to read and write fan fiction, including discussion elements and future story ideas

- **PlayStation Community**—allowing gamers to connect and talk with one another in forums, compete with friends for trophies, and provide user-generated content

- **Harley Owners Group (HOG)**—a way to connect fellow riders dedicated to the HOG lifestyle and brand. With over one million active members, the strength of the community lies in the openness and highly impassioned members it tries to foster and serve.

- **The SAP Community Network**—over 2.5 million engaged members contributing their time and expertise to develop SAP applications for their own businesses

The Internet makes it easy for anyone to run an online survey using a free tool like SurveyMonkey, Typeform, Google Forms, Zoho Survey, SurveyGizmo, SurveyPlanet, and others. That doesn't mean just *anyone* should. Flawed research outcomes can result from biased questions, poor question design, and small sample sizes.

Social media, of course, isn't the only way to get real-time insights. Observing customers in their natural environment can also be revealing and is becoming more and more prevalent. Some companies have turned to ethnographers—social scientists dedicated to studying people in their natural environments—as a means to uncover valuable insight and stories.

"If you want to understand how a lion hunts you don't go to the zoo, you go to the jungle," says David Sable, global chief executive of Y&R, a creative agency owned by WPP PLC. Ford Motor Company, L'Oreal, and Lloyds Bank, among others, are doing just that.

After Ford released its redesigned Mustang in the late 1990s, owners found the car to be less powerful than its original model, despite the fact that Ford had significantly increased the power of the car. By riding along with new Mustang owners, ethnographers found that power was more about the visceral experience than the vehicle's horsepower. Ford refashioned the car, along with its brand strategy, to appeal to the "irresponsible pleasure of youth" that the original Mustang delivered.[9]

At L'Oreal Australia, management believes that customer insight is not just the remit of a particular person who has "insights" in their job title, but rather that everyone—from the executive ranks to interns—need to be consumer centric. The company's Customer Connect program encourages all employees to take a day away from their regular roles to observe and talk to customers in their homes, shops, or other locations they frequent.[10] The insights create a continuous feedback loop that allows L'Oreal to make real-time adjustments versus engaging in a specific research project.

Lloyds Bank taps into its frontline employees for keen customer insight. When the UK bank was redesigning its mortgages, it gathered a group of its call center agents, without the presence of managers, and asked them to help identify problems that existed with their mortgage process. Within thirty minutes, the agents had identified the top ten problems facing customers. It took a data analysis team six weeks to analyze all of the customer and operational data to conclude that the agents were 80 percent right.[11]

Another method to obtain customer insights in real time is through events. Whether it's an industry event, trade show, executive retreat, or product launch, events continue to be a major avenue for building relationships, influencing attendees, and sharing industry thought leadership.[12] The unique aspect of events is that they can straddle the online and offline world. Rather than treat that next customer meeting as an isolated event, view it instead as part of a holistic and integrated marketing insights strategy.

And don't overlook *little data* as a rich source of customer insights. No tidbit of customer insight is too small to matter. While big data may be all the rage, little data about a customer's prior interactions, for example, might just be the key to improve the customer experience and make that next transaction more likely.[13] That's exactly what software company Intuit does. Intuit sells financial, accounting, and tax preparation software and related services for small businesses, accountants, and individuals. Even though the company has been around for more than three decades, it ranked #8 on *Fortune's* new Future 50 list of companies best prepared to thrive and grow their revenue rapidly in coming years. Part of Intuit's secret sauce is digging into little data that seems odd or nonsensical in order to find business-changing insights. The key, which Intuit has never forgotten, is to focus on the finding that makes no sense. Cofounder Scott Cook calls it "savoring the surprise," and it has enabled the company to reinvent itself before competitors catch on.[14]

Beyond Customer Insights

These customer insight methods can also be applied to gathering insights from other key constituencies—partners, investors, donors, suppliers, employees, and others.

It's fair to say that most companies know more about their customers than they do their own employees. With employee engagement now one of the top three concerns of most HR professionals (the other two being turnover and succession planning), companies are realizing that this isn't just an HR problem—it's a business problem.[15] Indeed, studies have linked stronger employee engagement to higher customer satisfaction and profits.[16]

John Deere & Company is a good example of a company that looks at its business holistically. Deere measures employee morale every two weeks—a huge departure from the annual or biennial employee satisfaction surveys and performance reviews of the past. Management at Deere believes employee motivation is as essential to its business as are operational and financial metrics and has built the frequent pulse into their two-week product development cycle. This allows them to identify and act immediately to correct process and motivational problems with people and teams in real time, which then translates to bringing new products and features to market sooner.[17]

A Single View of the Customer?

The end game for all marketers is to create a single database that houses everything their organization knows about each of its customers, putting it all in one place and making it accessible with a click. This will finally enable the shift away from mass marketing toward truly personalized marketing. Ashu Garg, general partner of Foundation Capital, describes it as the shift from connecting with a million people at once to connecting with one person—and doing it a million times over.[18]

Having a single view of the customer is a twenty-year old idea that has still not yet fully arrived . . . but we're getting closer.[19] "72 percent of customers understand the advantages of a single customer view, but only 16 percent (of UK businesses) have one in place," finds Experian, a UK data company.[20] So what's the holdup? Certainly the technology is there for those companies willing to invest in its capabilities.

Certainly the payback is there too. Watermark Consulting tracked the eight-year stock performance of *customer experience leaders* versus *customer experience laggards* versus the S&P 500. They found that the *leaders* outperformed the market, generating a total return that was thirty-five points higher than the S&P 500 Index. The *laggards* trailed far behind, posting a total return that was forty-five points lower than that of the broader market.[21] This is a striking reminder of how a great customer experience is rewarded over the long term by customers and investors alike.

Not surprisingly, the holdup is all the usual internal culprits: people, processes, siloes, priorities, tradeoffs, and management buy-in just to name a few. While customer experience is inching its way up in the list of management priorities, it hasn't made its way to the very top, at least not just yet. Perhaps that will change if what Ernan Roman, president of ERDM and author of *Voice-of-the-Customer Marketing*, predicts comes true: By 2020, customer experience will overtake price and product as the key brand differentiator.[22] That doesn't mean there aren't steps we can take now to accelerate the journey.

From Brand Ambassadors to Customer Champions

As marketing leaders, we need to be the champions for the customer. And that starts with customer insights. Business-to-consumer (B2C) CMOs have an advantage here. Consumer CMOs have a data-driven understanding of their customers and have used it to shape the buyer's journey.[23] This is not as prevalent in the B2B world, where companies have an enterprise sales force that knows the customer far better than the CMO does. That is slowly changing thanks to the rise of marketing automation, which now provides CMOs with the tools to adopt a B2C approach in working with B2B customers.

Granted, we don't own the end-to-end customer experience and all its touch points, but that doesn't mean we can't step up and lead the framework, standards, and transformation.

Here are some things marketing leaders can do to move their organizations toward what Jack Springman, director at Digital Springboard, calls "customer curiosity."

1. **Make customers a strategy:** Instead of just viewing customers as an audience, make them a strategy. Turn your marketing strategy into a customer strategy with VoC at its core.

2. **Get up close and personal:** Each quarter, spend a day traveling with one of your salespeople as they meet with customers or at a call center as agents interact with customers. Encourage your team members to do the same.

3. **Listen and learn:** Continually monitor and collect insights from across all your key constituencies. Invite employees to share ideas for improving the customer experience. Analyze the digital data trail from your customers' online and mobile interactions.

4. **Share insights broadly:** Aggregate and share customer feedback throughout your organization, not just the executive staff.

5. **Provide a daily dosage of insight:** Start each meeting with a review of newly learned customer (and employee) insights.

6. **Eat your own dog food:** Ensure your employees are using your company's products and services, if possible.

7. **Empower decisions:** Empower your employees to *bend the rules* on occasion when it is clearly in the best interest of the customer.

8. **Understand your customer's journey:** Map your customer's end-to-end journey to not only understand and better synchronize every touch point of the experience, but also to identify any gaps. Do this as a joint exercise with sales, support services, operations, product development, corporate strategy, finance, IT, and others.

9. **Be the change:** Use customer-friendly language on your website and in all your sales and marketing pieces. Model the behavior, and recognize others when they do too.

10. **Take (focused) action:** Not all feedback you receive is actionable or aligned with your company's core purpose. Develop a systemic way of filtering the insights you receive

and then take swift action on those that fit with your organization's strategy.

Summary

I often cringe when management consultants, data scientists, market researchers, and academics describe and define marketing roles and activities. But they might cringe as well at my worldview of *VoC, customer experience,* and *customer insights.* Admittedly, these are rich disciplines in which many professionals have invested their livelihoods, much like I have in marketing.

What I do know is this: Businesses that *know their customers* are better positioned to meet customer needs. This leads to better (and more cost-efficient) customer engagement yielding better results. I also know that insight without action is just idle chatter. We'll look at how companies can turn their newfound *listening and learning* into high-speed *execution and iteration* in the next chapter.

Chapter 3 Key Takeaways:

- Insights are your lifeline to the customer.

- Most businesses have rich customer insights but struggle to aggregate and activate those insights in real time.

- Executives have traditionally relied on a combination of quantitative data from surveys and qualitative insights from focus groups and interviews. New real-time methods can accelerate real-time decision making.

- Social media, online brand communities, observing customers in their natural environment, frontline employees, and physical events not only provide rich insights, they provide a platform for co-creation and dynamic customer engagement.

- Don't overlook the power of *little data*, those gems of insight that just might unlock richer customer understanding.

- Triangulating information from multiple sources will provide your organization with a continuous stream of customer insights and a knowledge-based competitive advantage.

- Customer insight methods can also be applied to other target audiences: partners, investors, donors, suppliers, and employees.

- Becoming an *insight machine* will better enable you to deliver a personalized, differentiated, and more cost-efficient customer experience.

- Marketing leaders must take a leadership role in transforming their cultures into being *customer-curious*.

Chapter 4

AGILITY IN ACTION

"Success today requires the agility and drive to constantly rethink, reinvigorate, react, and reinvent."
—Bill Gates

Chapter 3 showed us the many ways to become an insight machine. Insight, of course, is not an end point. Rather, it is a springboard to action. In this chapter we'll turn our newfound customer insight into actions that delight our customers and provide us with a competitive business advantage. Truth be told, the larger the company the harder it is to turn customer insight into customer experiences. But it doesn't have to be that way. We'll look at one brand, Oreo, that has successfully unlocked the secret to marketing agility. But before we do that, let's define *agility*.

For most of us, agility means the ability to move quickly and easily. It defines someone or something that is alert, sharp, light-footed, and nimble. Examples might include an agile mind, an agile athlete, an agile leap, or an agile person. In the world of software development, agility has come to take on a different meaning. Software application developers have adopted the term to describe a methodology and process for reducing the traditionally long lead times involved in developing software. By dividing a complex project into short phases of intensive work (sprints) with frequent progress assessments (daily scrums) and rapid adaptation, teams can now deliver software in a condensed timeframe.[1]

In recent years, that same rigor and process has been applied to marketing, predominantly digital, short-term, direct-response marketing campaigns. *Agile marketing* heavily focuses on marketing-technology infrastructure and process (*martech*), fueled by data and analytics.

The *marketing agility* I'm advocating doesn't involve sprints, scrums, or scrum masters. Instead of technology infrastructure and process, marketing agility emphasizes people and organizations. Marketing agility applies equally to traditional and digital methods, as well as to demand generation and brand building. It is an organizational capability as well as a professional attribute.

That's not to say that *agile marketing* and *marketing agility* don't share some of the same underlying beliefs. They do. They both emphasize and embrace a willingness to iterate, adapt, and change in real-time based on results, new information, or insight. Aside from sharing agility as their strategic intent, the two concepts are quite different.

What we'll cover next are the three main pillars of marketing agility: *organizational agility*, *personal agility*, and *learning agility*.

Organizational Agility: Agility of All

In Chapter 2, we looked at a number of factors that caused organizations to initiate a reset or a complete business transformation. They included a company's natural maturation, technology disruption, entry of a new market player, a competitive advance, business or market fluctuations, industry consolidation, an acquisition or merger, shifting business priorities, and a new generation of consumers with new demands. In each instance, change was not an option. Rather, it was a matter of business survival. How well a company responds to external factors has a lot to do with its organizational agility.

Organizational agility is a measure of how quickly an organization can change direction when the situation demands and still remain robust enough to absorb any setbacks.

The term *agility* has been applied to many aspects of a business. It extends to operations (*process agility, manufacturing agility, supply chain agility*), to products (*portfolio agility, service agility, systems agility*), to leadership (*strategic agility, team agility, emotional agility*) and more. Larry Cooper, who leads an agility LinkedIn group, cuts through it all: "Organizational agility is what you get when all the other types of agility are present."[2]

Despite its pervasiveness, a 2016 survey by American Productivity & Quality Center (APQC) found that while most businesses considered organizational agility "important" (51 percent) or "extremely important" (38 percent), most were better at identifying opportunities and risks (strategic responsiveness) than in executing on them (organizational flexibility). So that begets the question: If agility is so universally understood and widely embraced, why have so few companies mastered it?

APQC identifies five top challenges to achieving organizational flexibility:

(1) Operational silos

(2) Organizational resistance

(3) Slow decision making

(4) Unaligned processes, and

(5) Poor knowledge management

APQC and others also offer ways we can address these obstacles, including:

- A planning process that is cross-functional and fluid

- The use of strong dashboards and balanced scorecards

- Effective and transparent communications that encourage engagement

- An increased comfort level for risk and rewards for those who take them

- Incentives for frontline employees in their dealings with customers

- Ready access to trusted and relevant information

- More effective knowledge management systems embedded in employees' flow of work[3]

It goes without saying that organizational agility is best when it is applied across an entire company, but that doesn't mean we can't jumpstart it within our own marketing departments. Let's take a look at what *marketing agility in action* looks like.

The Marketing Agility Needed to Seize an Oreo Moment

When the power went out in New Orleans in 2013 during Super Bowl XLVII (47), Oreo proclaimed in a perfectly timed tweet: "Power out? No problem. You can still dunk in the dark." The tweet quickly became one of the most buzz-worthy ads of the Super Bowl, and it wasn't even a commercial. Many may think it was a streak of in-the-moment marketing brilliance. It actually was a result of Oreo's marketing agility.

Oreo had a mission control center (aka war room) set up within their agency when the blackout happened. About fifteen people worked on the tweet and accompanying image (including the legal team and the communications team), and it was approved and ready to launch within minutes of the actual blackout. Talk about real-time marketing!

Lisa Mann, then VP of Cookies, said, "Everyone thinks it just happened." In reality, that tweet took two years of preparation.

Oreo had a well-oiled social media team with a process and empowerment to implement a major message like this in minutes, instead of days. The tweet quickly became one of the most memorable ad moments of the game, earning more than 10,000 retweets and making headlines in more than 100 countries. Oreo's *keen insight* and *nimble activation* set a new benchmark for marketing agility on one of the world's most visible stages.

Marketing agility is not the speed at which you execute your marketing campaigns. Rather, it is the speed at which you can take real-time customer insight and turn it into *moments of truth* in the customer's buying journey.

Do you want to create *Oreo moments* for your own company? You can, by adopting the following four marketing best practices that Oreo exemplified:

(1) Building a strong cross-functional team with clear roles

(2) Crafting a streamlined and agreed-to approval process

(3) Continuously monitoring trends, news, and events for opportunities to have a customer dialogue, and

(4) Creating a culture that encourages calculated risk taking and that rewards rapid decision taking

To remain relevant and competitive, we need to tap into everyday customer moments with creativity, authenticity, and speed. That doesn't mean resigning ourselves to seat-of-the-pants marketing. To the contrary, it requires even more vision, strategy, preparation, and coordination than ever before.

Personal Agility: Agility of One

Let's ladder-down from the agility of all to the agility of one: *personal agility*. As Gary Hamel, a management educator and business thinker, reminds us: "You can't build an adaptable organization without adaptable people."

With the very nature of organizations and world of work rapidly changing, what is it that we need to adapt to? And what are those things that we can do, personally, to increase our agility as marketing professionals? To answer the first question, let's look at the top ten workplace trends predicted by Dan Schawbel, partner and research director at Future Workplace.[4] This will help us better understand the areas where we might need to *dial up* our current knowledge, processes and practices.

1. **Companies will focus on improving their candidate and employee experiences.** With the increasing war for talent, creating an employment experience for job seekers and candidates can no longer be ignored.

2. **The blended workforce is on the rise.** Companies are increasingly hiring on-demand freelancers to work alongside their permanent employees as a way to solve key problems and reduce costs in the form of healthcare coverage and benefits.

3. **Annual performance reviews are evolving into more continuous reviews.** The annual performance review process is being abolished as younger employees demand instant feedback and course correction. Two of the largest companies in the world, GE and Adobe, have already nixed their annual review process in exchange for providing regular employee feedback.

4. **Millennials meet Generation Z in the workplace.** This blending will widen the technology gap even more between younger and older workers.

5. **Augmented and virtual reality will revolutionize recruiting and training.** The technology that employees are experiencing outside of work will naturally influence them to desire the same tech at the office, resulting in employee training that is more engaging, less expensive, and free of distractions.

6. **The war for talent will heat up as the employer and employee contract continues to evolve.** The average tenure for US employees, regardless of age, is a mere 4.6 years, evidence of the continued migration away from lifetime employment.

7. **Organizations will restructure to focus on team over individual performance.** Ninety-two percent of companies rate *organizational design* as their top priority, acknowledging that high-performing teams will enable companies to compete for the future.

8. **Workplace wellness and well-being will become critical employee benefits for attracting top talent.** Companies realize that workplace stress is the biggest health issue employees face and are investing in creating more relaxing and healthier environments.

9. **Companies will get creative with their employee benefit packages and perks.** Once you get past pay, the two most important benefits employees cite are healthcare coverage and work flexibility.

10. **Office attire and workplace culture are becoming more casual.** Today, 50 percent of managers say that employees wear less formal clothing than they did five years ago and nearly one-third of employees would prefer to be at a company with a *business-casual* dress code.

No doubt about it, that's a lot of change in the workplace and in the way work gets done in the future. There will be new technologies, new coworkers, new performance measures, new employee contracts, new perks, new dress codes—and shorter tenures.

So how do we not only survive but thrive and succeed in this new work environment? The short answer is to develop our personal and professional agility. There are structured ways of cultivating and measuring agility, as well as less formal and unstructured methods. We'll look at both.

The National Research Council (NRC), the Government of Canada's premier research organization, developed a five-point scale to evaluate an employee's personal agility competency.[5] It progresses from Level 1, "changes when required," to Level 5, "enables an environment that fosters personal agility." At the lower levels of personal agility, employees adapt to new approaches when explained *why* and *how* while maintaining a positive outlook as pressure increases. At each progressive level, employees are evaluated on how proactively they model their own change behaviors as well as how they encourage and create an agile work environment. You can download a copy of the NRC's personal agility five-point scale from my website, www.marketingflexology.com.

NRC's competency model is excellent for defining, measuring, and evaluating personal and professional agility across a large group of employees. Additionally, it sends a message to the organization that agility is valued as a core leadership trait. But you don't need to wait for a companywide mandate to get started. There are things you can do starting today to increase your personal and professional agility. They include the *power of association*, the *power of experience*, and the *power of yes*.

Developing Personal Agility: The Power of Association

Jim Rohn, author and motivational speaker, wisely notes: "You are the average of the five people you spend the most time with." Rather than adapt to the environment in which you find yourself (Level 1 of the NRC agility scale), you can proactively choose to change or create your ideal environment. Surrounding yourself with people whose traits you admire and from whom you can learn is what I call the *power of association*. Consciously and subconsciously, their actions and behaviors will influence your everyday choices.

While we can't always pick our family, boss, or CEO, we certainly can choose the employees we hire, the suppliers we work with, the teams we form, the coworkers we have lunch with or hang out with after work, the people we mentor and who mentor us, and the professional associations to which we belong, among others.

If you want to develop your personal and professional agility, surround yourself with colleagues who have a track record for successfully challenging the status quo without being perceived as rabble-rousers. The power of association is very effective and completely within our control.

Developing Personal Agility: The Power of Experience

The second action you can take to increase your personal and professional agility is to seek out new experiences and perspectives. New experiences, especially those that are challenging or even a bit uncomfortable, can stretch you in new ways. This doesn't necessarily mean switching companies or changing careers, though these options are also viable. If you are a career marketing professional, you can seek out a number of new experiences within your chosen profession.

For example, if you work behind the scenes in a marketing operations or automation role, pursuing a customer-centric position can help you gain valuable up-close-and-personal insight into customers. If your marketing positions to date have been strictly US based, seeking out experience in different parts of the world can expose you to new buying habits, workplace practices, and customs. If you've been at corporate headquarters for many years where long-term planning and governance are valued, switching to a product group can help you develop experimentation and high-speed iteration skills. If you support a business group with quarterly sales in the tens of millions, rotating to support a struggling startup division will help keep you nimble.

These are just a few of the many ways you can purposefully choose to expand your experience and perspective. In the words of the late Oliver Wendell Holmes Jr.: "A mind that is stretched by a new experience can never go back to its old dimensions." That is why experiences are a powerful and proven way to enhance your personal and professional agility.

Developing Personal Agility: The Power of Yes

The third method for increasing your personal and professional agility is to develop the habit of raising your hand. Whether it's tackling a current business obstacle or seizing upon a new growth opportunity, companies are never short on things to do. They do, however, often struggle to find the resources to get it all done. That's why managers generally welcome it when employees volunteer to either lead an initiative, take part on a project team, participate in a brainstorming session, or otherwise offer their time and expertise to assist.

There are times when we raise our hand and other times when we are drafted. Over my own career, I frequently served as a volunteer *and* a draft pick for special assignments. Most of the time, I willingly accepted. Some assignments were company-wide initiatives; others were leading a project management office (PMO). Some took me out of marketing; others put me squarely in the center of transforming marketing. Some were full-time assignments; others were in addition to current duties. And, yes, some were downright dogs. But all of them were tremendous opportunities to develop new leadership skills while having an active hand in designing and implementing an initiative management had deemed important. Each new assignment provided opportunities to observe, listen, ask, and learn. They gave me new insights, perspective, and skills. And, by doing so, they raised my personal and professional agility.

Let me share with you an example to illustrate what I mean. Several years back, I was running corporate marketing for HP's

Americas Region when my good colleague in the Asia-Pacific Region left the company. My boss, the chief marketing officer, asked me to step in and "keep things humming" across Asia-Pacific while simultaneously assessing the existing marketing talent. I felt like I had just added a night job to my current day job; in hindsight, this experience stretched me in career-beneficial ways.[6]

The next six months were crazy: the time zones, the travel, and of course the extra hours. I personally met with every member of the Asia-Pacific marketing team along with internal business clients and agency partners. In response, I made some key staffing changes over the next several months, eliminated redundant positions, and recruited and on-boarded a new regional marketing VP. Not only did the assignment give me new perspective and appreciation for the culture and challenges faced in another part of the world, but it also fostered greater understanding and ties between our two regions. Most importantly, it made me a more agile leader, which I carried with me to my future management positions.

Agility is an extremely valuable leadership trait, particularly in times of change and uncertainty. Start building your personal and professional agility today by practicing the *power of association*, *the power of experience*, and the *power of yes*.

Learning Agility: Agility Forever

The third key pillar of marketing agility is learning agility. *Learning agility* has been described as lifelong learning, the leadership skill for a moving target, learning something new, or unlearning something old. Microsoft's US marketing chief, Grad Conn, sums it up this way: "Pretend you're in school for the rest of your life."[7] Regardless of how you define learning agility, it is clearly considered an essential leadership skill.

Korn Ferry has conducted more than 2.5 million leadership assessments over the past four decades. They found that being *learning agile* is a key predictor of success and a critical attribute of effective breakthrough leadership, above intelligence, education level, or even leadership competencies. Yet only 15 percent of executives possess this trait.[8]

To succeed as a marketing leader in today's *faster is the new fast* world, we have no choice but to master our ability to adapt and learn. Microsoft's Conn describes marketing as "a profession that requires continuous study and investment if you are going to have any hope in staying at pace with it. What you learned yesterday is already old news."

Sometimes we are fortunate enough to work for a company that promotes and invests in continuous learning, like AT&T. AT&T is in the midst of what might be the most ambitious retraining program in corporate American history. Dubbed Workforce 2020, the initiative plans to retrain 100,000 AT&T employees (nearly a third of its global workforce) to be technically proficient by 2020, and the company is investing $1 billion to do so.[9]

The retraining initiative combines online and classroom-based course work in subjects like digital networking and data science—skills AT&T has identified as crucial to its cloud-heavy future. AT&T chairman and CEO Randall Stephenson says, "There is a need to retool yourself, and you should not expect to stop. People who do not spend five to ten hours a week in online learning will obsolete themselves with the technology."

Governments are also encouraging the adoption of new, in-demand skills to safeguard their country's continued growth and prosperity. The government of Singapore is incentivizing its citizens to stay ahead of technology change by giving vouchers worth a few hundred dollars to each adult over twenty-five. They can use them to pay for online training from more than 500 approved providers.[10]

Additionally, Singapore is working with Google to train 1,000 business leaders of small- and medium-size enterprises in digital leadership by 2019. Similarly, the Royal Bank of Canada launched a ten-year $500-million commitment to help young Canadians prepare for the future of work by addressing three critical gaps: experience, skills, and networking.[11]

Even Silicon Valley is feeling the pinch and getting into the act. To plug the shortfall in qualified workers, executives from Facebook, Google, LinkedIn, and other big tech companies are partnering with a private university to train people in the skills needed to land new high-paying jobs in the digital economy. Graduates of the new private-public partnership learn about design and UX, social networks, ecommerce, search engines, and digital law and, at the end of the nine-month program, receive a Master's Degree in Internet Business. An expert in the field teaches each module from a partnering Silicon Valley tech company.[12]

But what are companies doing to train the next level of agile marketing leaders? There's some good news on that front as well.

A 2016 study of US-based executive recruiters across nineteen search firms ranked the best companies for developing C-level marketing leaders.[13] Not surprisingly, the majority are consumer-packaged goods (CPG) companies, with Procter & Gamble leading the pack. P&G's systematic and disciplined profit-and-loss (P&L) training, its emphasis on holding marketers accountable for total business results, and its track record for developing successful C-level leaders put it at the top of the list. P&G's brand management organization, specifically, has proven to be a great training ground for not just marketing execs, but also for other C-suite positions.

All of the top fifteen companies in the study had a long track record of developing marketing talent internally, versus bringing talent in from the outside. Two technology companies made the top fifteen list—Apple at #8 and Amazon at #13. This is significant because tech companies have not yet shown a sustained commitment to developing marketing talent.

Bear in mind, all of these examples are exceptions rather than the rule. According to research by Wharton School professor Peter Cappelli, in general, businesses provide less employee training than they previously did. In 1979, the average young worker received 2.5 weeks per year of training; a few decades later, the average had fallen to just eleven hours.

As a result, employees must take it upon themselves to increase their knowledge base and upgrade their skills, and apparently many are. According to *Forbes*, online learning became a $100-billion-per-year industry in 2015, and it still shows no signs of slowing down. Learning is no longer something we just do in schools; learning agility is something today's successful marketers embrace to outsmart change and future-proof their careers.

Summary

Marketing agility is not the speed at which we execute our marketing campaigns. It is not an excuse for being flighty, unfocused or, worse, in perpetual pursuit of bright, shiny new ideas. Rather, marketing agility is the speed and timeliness with which we can take real-time customer insight and turn it into *Oreo moments*. The windows when a customer takes action are small and few. We must be prepared to seize those moments of truth.

Preparation requires marketing agility—individuals and organizations that are nimble, lean, adaptive, learning, and committed to high-speed execution and iteration.

Chapter 4 Key Takeaways:

- *Agile marketing* and *marketing agility* are often confused and used interchangeably. While they share some underlying beliefs, they are not one and the same.

- To become a more agile marketer, we need to develop greater organizational agility, personal agility, and lifelong learning agility.

- Don't confuse marketing agility with seat-of-the-pants marketing. Marketing agility requires vision, strategy, preparation, and coordination.

- You can accelerate your personal agility through the *power of association*, the *power of experience*, and the *power of yes*.

- Agility is an extremely valuable trait during times of uncertainty and change. Embracing marketing agility can future-proof your career.

Chapter 5

THE MARKETING SHAKE(UP)

"Your life does not get better by chance, it gets better by change."
—Jim Rohn

Thus far we've covered two of the essential ingredients required for modern marketing success: *insight* and *agility*. The need for high-speed listening, learning, execution, and iteration has never been greater, yet the marketing profession has never been on less solid footing. So that begs the question: Where do we go from here?

Columnist and marketing professor Mark Ritson believes it's hard for marketers to be sure of anything these days. "It has never been a more exhilarating or exhausting time to work in this discipline. Never before has so much happened in marketing with so little consensus around what is and isn't working. We do our business on what appears to be a continually moving and undulating platform of knowledge that constantly contradicts and reverses itself as we cling on for grim life."[1]

That is why my recipe for *Marketing Flexology* includes *shake well* in its instructions. Getting into the habit of routinely scrutinizing your marketing investments and results helps avoid complacency and better prepares you and your team for the inevitable reinvention. Consider these challenging realities:

1. **Short Tenures:** Executive search firm Spencer Stuart reports the average CMO tenure among consumer brands

fell to 3.5 years in 2016, citing tough business headwinds, new technologies, and pressures to change quickly. In comparison, CEO tenure was 7.2 years among the S&P 500, while CFO tenure was 5.7 years among the Fortune 500.[2]

2. **Invisible on Boards:** Of the roughly 9,800 board seats held within Fortune 1000 companies, marketers occupy a scant sixty-eight.[3]

3. **First to Blame:** CMOs are the most likely among the C-suite to get axed when growth targets are missed.[4]

4. **Undervalued:** In survey after survey, marketing is listed as one of the least valuable professions to humanity, scraping the bottom alongside politicians and civil servants.[5]

5. **No Professional Code:** Marketing operates largely under voluntary and self-regulating principles that go (slightly) beyond a company's legal obligations. Our profession has no unifying code of conduct (other than slow-to-react and open-to-interpretation Federal Trade Commission rulings).[6] Nor do we have a professional designation, certification, or recertification process, as do doctors, accountants, and lawyers.

6. **Lack of Standard Reporting:** Nearly every business function—sales, legal, operations, finance—has a *generally accepted* or legally mandated standard for reporting results. Marketing does not, hurting our ability to justify and compete on an equal footing for continued investment.

7. **Tension between CEO and CMO:** 80 percent of CEOs don't trust or are unimpressed with their CMOs (ouch!). In comparison, just 10 percent of the same CEOs feel that way about their CFOs and CIOs.[7]

8. **Tension among Practitioners:** Marketers are not a particularly cohesive lot. There's little consensus among us on what constitutes marketing best practices, accompanied by a continual jousting over resources and budgets. You find advocates *and* cynics for inbound versus outbound

marketing, brand building versus demand generation, paid versus earned versus owned media, and traditional versus digital channels.

Despite the odds, business degrees (including marketing, business, and management) continue to be a popular career choice with one in five US college grads receiving a bachelor's degree in this field each year.[8] This is in addition to the current 10.6 million professionals worldwide who list *marketing* or *marketer* in their LinkedIn job title. The market demand is keeping pace, with nearly all sectors of marketing slated to grow between 5 and 9 percent over the next several years, according to the Bureau of Labor Statistics.[9] And salaries continue to look rewarding, with median annual wages holding steady between $95,000 and $130,000 (USD) per year.

This goes to show that marketers are not easily deterred. The adventure and excitement of our field has long been the allure that attracts the most imaginative, innovative, pioneering, and boundary-pushing talent.[10] The best way for marketers to cope with the inevitable *shake* is to be prepared, nimble, and flexible, and to never get too comfortable along the way.

Riding the Marketing Rollercoaster

There's no avoiding or eliminating the 4Ms of organization change, which we covered in Chapter 2. A management change, entry of a new market player, an acquisition or divestiture, a disappointing quarter, or simply a new direction for the company can all lead to upheaval in our best-laid marketing plans. And it usually results in a *marketing transformation*.

Marketing transformations go by many names—reinventions, realignments, revamps, readjustments, refreshes, restructurings. They typically mean one thing: *reduce*. Without a doubt, marketing transformations are hugely disruptive. Instead of inspiring thoughts of increased efficiency, effectiveness, and positive change, restructurings generate distrust, anxiety, and often work paralysis. Worse, they shift our focus away from serving customers toward *fixing* our internal affairs. *But how we respond to the unexpected upheaval can determine our success or failure.*

There are three typical reactions during a transformation: *fight, flight,* or *freeze.* Some people react to change with a vengeance (*fight*). They don't accept what's *going down* and may even hide information or resources. Some become subversive in an attempt to hold on to their perceived power, budgets, departments, and positions. They build small power bases with other like-minded employees and plot how to undermine the planned changes. These are the *change saboteurs.*

Some employees react to change by seeking out other, potentially more stable opportunities (*flight*). This group tends to be the most confident and employable people in your company. They know their skills are valuable and will take them elsewhere if provoked or stalled. These employees typically are your high-potential employees and represent a flight risk during a transition.

There is a third group of employees who react to change like a deer in the headlights (*freeze*). They are paralyzed by change and obsess over the potential consequences and outcomes. They keep their heads down, waiting for things to return to *normal,* praying they still have a job when it does. Or they may become so shaken that they spend countless hours *trading information* with coworkers about who's in and who's out—to the detriment of their performance and customers. These employees feel helpless and unempowered.

Recognizing and understanding how you and your coworkers react to stressful situations can help you avert detrimental consequences, including:

(1) Resistance and subversion

(2) Potential loss of top talent

(3) Performance paralysis

There are even more proactive ways to survive—and even thrive from—a marketing transformation. The quotation "never let a good crisis go to waste" has been attributed to Winston Churchill (though there is some doubt as to whether he actually used those words). This quote points to the fact that in times of crisis, there is more latitude to question an existing process, propose a new idea, establish a new norm, or demonstrate leadership. Understanding that, here are some tips to tackle that next marketing upheaval head-on:

1. **Engage:** The calmest weather is often found at the center of a hurricane or tropical storm, making it the safest place to be. As with a hurricane, the winds of change blow more fiercely at the edges of a transformation. Choose to be in the eye of the storm, where the weather is usually still and calm. You can do this by volunteering to lead or participate in a project management office or reinvention work stream. That way, you get a voice in the organization redesign.

2. **Be Forthright:** Don't hide information or resources. The first step in most reinventions is establishing a starting baseline that frames the current-state situation, including budgets, programs, agencies, head count, contractors, metrics, processes, best practices, and the like. This is not a time to play hide and seek or to *reclassify* employees into other safer job categories. This is a time to get on board and do what's right for the long-term viability of your company.

3. **Offer Suggestions:** This is a time to provide constructive input and offer up any best practices within your business, function, or geography to those leading the reinvention.

Most transformations aren't looking to reinvent the wheel; rather, they look for quick wins and *adopt-and-go* best practices that can be broadened across the company. In the same vein, be open to new ideas.

4. **Get on Board:** Don't react to a marketing reinvention with *fight, flight,* or *freeze.* Become an active partner in your company's marketing transformation, not a helpless victim. Change is difficult for most people, but the alternatives usually aren't very rosy.

5. **Be Courageous:** Challenging the status quo is scary *and* courageous. But it is the only way you can find new and better ways of doing things on behalf of your customers and company. Is there an outdated process that needs fixing? An agency relationship you should have exited long ago? A sponsorship that isn't adding sufficient value? Perhaps a long-running campaign that is underperforming? Always question *what* you are delivering and *how* you are delivering it. That's a surefire way to add value and exert leadership.

Shake or Be Shaken

The best way to avert change, of course, is to initiate it. This fact is substantiated by research by advisory services company Corporate Executive Board (now part of Gartner). It found that the highest contribution to the enterprise comes not from those who manage change when it happens to them, but from those who identify problems and related necessary changes *before they happen.* Employees who initiate change have a 43 percent more positive impact on their companies than those who just have the capacity to change.[11]

The enlightened marketing leader knows that the best reinventions are self-imposed, not other-imposed. They change the rules before someone else does. They know that they really only have two choices: to transform or to be transformed. And they act accordingly. The enlightened marketing leader takes to heart the words of the late President John F. Kennedy, who said, "The best time to repair the roof is when the sun is shining." They act preemptively, not reactively.

The enlightened marketing leader does the following:

- ✓ *Brings in outside talent in areas where the organization has gaps or needs in order to expand to stay relevant. It could be new marketing vehicles, new customer sets, or new marketing technologies. The leader also has a handful of continuous improvement initiatives underway at all times, putting him or her in the driver's seat.*

- ✓ *Keeps a tight rein on four dials—people, programs, budgets, and agencies—and doesn't wait until the dials are out-of-sync to take action.*

- ✓ *Builds a strong Marketing Flexology foundation that can withstand most any crisis du jour. That foundation is nimble (dexterous in movement and thought), lean (no superfluous fat), effective (gets the right things done), accountable (responsive and responsible), and learning (committed to continuous improvement).*

Adopting a learning mindset, building a flexible marketing capability, and keeping a keen eye on people-programs-budgets-agencies can help preempt the need for a major reinvention initiative. When your company *does* experience a leadership change, an acquisition or spin-off, or a competitive advance or market fluctuation, you'll be able to make the needed changes quickly while staying focused on producing brilliant marketing that engages customers. I talk more about the underlying foundation, dials, and tools of a *Marketing Flexology* organization in the chapters that follow.

When You Inherit a Mess

Initiating change within your existing company, organization, or team has its unique challenges, but it also has the benefit of acquired knowledge. What happens when you're joining a new company, transitioning to a new department, or inheriting a new team that's in disarray? How quickly should you make changes? Do you clean house on day one or wait six months until you've thoroughly learned the company and evaluated the organization? Obviously, there is no right or wrong answer.

A ten-year longitudinal study by leadership consulting firm Navalent on executive transitions found that more than 50 percent of executives who inherit a mess fail within their first eighteen months on the job.[12] This is particularly true when you arrive as an outsider and people you probably don't know created the mess.

Navalent offers these six tips to avoid failing in a new role:

1. Resist the temptation to emotionally distance yourself for fear of being implicated in the mess. Avoid using third-person references—they, them, those people. Use first-person references instead—we, our, us.

2. Never blame your predecessor; take the high road. Instead of focusing on the blunders of the past, focus on the changes going forward.

3. Minimize references to your past successes. Obviously, you were hired into this role because you had relevant past experiences. Odds are your entire team read about them when they checked you out.

4. Know the fine line between self-promotion (accompanied with personal agendas) and offers of real help from your team. Avoid the inevitable end-runs by providing opportunities for members of your team to share ideas with the entire group.

5. Test the reliability of your data and dueling fact bases to allow for more confident priority setting. External analysts and independent audits can be useful here.

6. Be transparent about how you will assess the organization and make changes and in what timeframe. *Leading out loud* helps you quickly build transparency and trust and reduce anxiety.

Above all, make sure you don't leave the place a bigger mess!

Summary

It is indeed baffling that there are marketing leaders still waiting for things to settle down and return to *normal*. It's not going to happen. Constant change *is* the new normal. While marketing reinventions and change initiatives may be unpredictable, they are inevitable. How we respond can determine our success or failure.

The best way to avert change is to initiate it. The question becomes: Will you shake up the status quo, or will you wait to be shaken? Consider the words of Seth Godin: "Increasingly, there are only two kinds of companies: brave and dead." That choice is yours.

Chapter 5 Key Takeaways:

- Marketing is a volatile yet exhilarating profession.

- Marketing reinventions, transformations, and change initiatives may be unpredictable, but they are inevitable. Preparation is your best response.

- Recognizing the three typical reactions to change—*fight, flight, freeze*—can help you avoid (1) change resistance and subversion, (2) potential loss of top talent, and (3) performance paralysis.

- While we often call crisis an *opportunity*, in reality it is a failure of management. There are more effective alternatives to riding the marketing reinvention rollercoaster.

- Putting *Marketing Flexology* into practice can ensure career stability and longevity.

Chapter 6

A SPLASH OF CREATIVITY

"Creativity is intelligence having fun."
—*Albert Einstein*

In the previous chapter, we covered ways to not only survive, but thrive from a marketing transformation. Challenging the status quo is the only way to find new and better solutions for our customers and our companies. However, doing so requires courage and some creativity.

In this chapter, we add the finishing touch to the *Marketing Flexology* mix we've stirred up thus far by adding in a *splash of creativity*. We'll examine the strong connection between creativity and business results and explore ways to ignite and foster creativity within our companies, teams, and selves through daily practice. We'll also look at how creativity just might save our profession from being replaced by robots.

Creativity is, and has always been, a critical component of successful marketing. It's how we break through the clutter, capture the attention of someone, give life to and differentiate our products and services, and then motivate a consumer toward action.

Back in my elementary school days, our fourth grade teacher regularly called out anyone who acted up in class as an *attention-getter*. I came to believe that attracting attention was a bad thing and to be avoided at all costs, lest you be chastised. In reality, it was Sister Theonita's way of squelching aberrant behavior in the classroom.

Years later, attention getting took on a different meaning as I began my career in public relations. The attention-getter, or hook, was critical to grabbing a reader's (or buyer's) interest. It's why newspapers use headlines, articles use imagery, and brands use logos. Some people and companies take attention-getting to an extreme, believing that any publicity is good publicity. Hence the maxim "It doesn't matter what they say about me, as long as they spell my name right."

Fast-forward several decades. Now, gaining the attention of today's consumer is often cited as a marketer's biggest challenge. In fact, a 2015 study conducted by Microsoft found that since the mobile revolution began, people now generally lose concentration after eight seconds—down from twelve seconds in 2000—which is one second less than the attention span of a goldfish![1]

Of course, grabbing attention should never be our primary creative goal. We've all seen brands—and people—do and say things simply to stand out and break through the clutter, using techniques that border on the shocking, tacky, bizarre, or foul-mouthed. That's what Sister Theonita would single out as an *attention-getter*. The attention getting I'm espousing is marketing creativity.

But Does Creativity Drive Sales?

No one disputes, and many studies have confirmed, that creative messages do in fact capture our attention. For example, it's been proven that creatively-awarded campaigns deliver eleven times the return on investment (ROI) of non-creatively awarded campaigns.[2] Yet, the connection between creativity and sales has been near impossible to prove. A few studies have brought us closer.

Adobe commissioned Forrester Consulting to quantify and qualify how creativity impacts business results. Surveying senior managers from corporations across a diverse set of industries, the study found that 82 percent of companies believe there is a strong connection between the two: Companies that are more creative gain greater business benefits, like revenue growth and market share.[3] Further, the report found companies that actively fostered creative thinking outperformed their peers and competitors in revenue growth, market share, and talent acquisition.

Similarly, the *Harvard Business Review* looked at which dimensions of creativity were more effective than others in influencing purchasing behavior.[4] Their study found that businesses realize higher sales when they use these five creativity techniques:

1. Originality (rare and surprising or that move away from the obvious and commonplace)

2. Flexibility (range of uses or ideas for the product or service)

3. Elaboration (unexpected details that extend the idea)

4. Synthesis (blending or connecting normally unrelated objects or ideas to create a divergent storyline)

5. Artistic value (aesthetically appealing verbal, visual, or sound elements)

Although all five elements had a positive impact on sales, elaboration had by far the most powerful impact, followed by artistic value. Trailing behind were originality and flexibility, with synthesis a distant fifth. Furthermore, the study found that combining elaboration with originality had almost double the average impact on sales, closely followed by the combination of artistic value and originality. In essence, being original is not enough—originality boosts sales only in the presence of additional creative dimensions. *Yet despite the direct correlation between creativity and business results, marketers today are flocking to data and analytics, rather than honing their creative chops.*

Perhaps that should come as no surprise. Today's CMO is under intense pressure to drive growth and justify the ROI of their marketing budget. Given the pressure to prove their value and financial contribution to their organizations, marketing leaders are increasingly turning to technology.

Has the Marketing Pendulum Swung Too Far?

In the early days of marketing, the goal was creative brilliance. In the 1950s—the golden age of creativity—marketers spent the majority of their budget on advertising and media. Fast-forward sixty years and companies now spend more on marketing technology than on advertising, rivaling what IT departments spend on technology.[5]

Over the past decade alone, the marketing pendulum has swung toward data and analytics. Indeed, data science is having a moment. *Wired* magazine suggests data science (a subset of the larger analytics discipline) is a more lucrative career track than medicine.[6] And heavyweight industry analysts Gartner and McKinsey put out research reports within a year of one another that project a shortfall of between 100,000 and 190,000 data science jobs by the end of the decade.[7] Our digital economy has become so dependent on big data that data science jobs now demand a premium. The *Harvard Business Review* called it "the sexiest job of the 21st century."[8]

Data and analytics have also spawned an entirely new marketing industry—dubbed *martech*—along with new capabilities, tools, and job titles. The number of martech offerings now tips the scale at a whopping 5,381 (from 4,891 unique companies).[9] Indeed, there is no shortage of sophisticated martech solutions available, all of which promise to make our marketing simpler, easier, and improve results. And companies are quickly adopting these solutions. On average, companies today are using a dozen or more marketing automation and data analytics tools. Frankly, that's crazy and unsustainable.

With all the new toys we've been given, CEOs and CFOs assume that marketing can now unearth even *more* new business opportunities, growth, and customers for their companies. Some have even bestowed CMOs with the added title of *chief growth officer*. For the first time, at the push of a proverbial button, marketers can now access rich data. No longer do we have to sheepishly admit, as marketing pioneer John Wanamaker did, that "Half the money I spend on advertising is wasted; the trouble is, I don't know which half." Marketing automation and big data tell us when impressions are up, click-through rates are holding steady, bounce rates are improving, and share of voice is tanking.

However, there is a flip side to having too much data at our fingertips.

First and foremost, it can lead to *analysis paralysis*. Having too much information sometimes overcomplicates and delays a decision that could be, and should be, quite simple.

Second, an over-focus on data can marginalize creativity. Creative elements, such as content, headlines, and visuals, merely become additional elements to test. Fritz Brumder, CEO and cofounder of Brandlive, said it well: "Digital marketing has become a world where data often overruns the creative process. A/B (or even A/B/C/D) testing every element in a campaign becomes the obsession, relegating the ideas to simply more variables to test."[10]

And finally, an overreliance on technology can make us forget that we're marketing to people, not to numbers.[11] Too many marketers spend too much of their time behind computer screens treating people like variables in a formula rather than trying to get inside their hearts, minds, and motivations. Sure, your winning campaign may have the greatest click-through rates, but unless you know *why*, it's difficult to replicate and scale.

There's More to Marketing than Data

Martech, and its sibling Adtech, work best with short-lived online marketing campaigns that have a specified start and end date. But not all marketing is digital, not all marketing is programmatic, and not all marketing is focused on driving demand through a pipeline.

For example, martech isn't very good at measuring nondigital, awareness-generating activities. These include the effectiveness of your long-term brand building, reputation management, strategic relationships (media, analyst, partners, and others), product strategies, the strength of your sales and marketing relationship, and your end-to-end customer experience.

There's still a lot to be said for up-close-and-personal marketing, street-smart public relations, and working the crowd at an event. I don't know of any campaign that *went viral* as a result of an algorithm. Building relationships builds reputations and brands—something a formula can't do. Touching upon a key truth, keen insight, unfulfilled need, or even a raw nerve produces far greater and lasting impact than any technology can deliver. And that's the creativity twist of *Marketing Flexology*. The ability to ask smart questions, think creatively, and act strategically can't be replicated by big data or marketing automation technologies (at least for now). As such, creativity is marketing's best career insurance.

Creative Jobs Are Hard to Automate

Artificial intelligence, or AI, is certainly poised to transform marketing as we know it today. If we can produce self-driving cars, then what's to prevent us from developing self-driving marketing campaigns? Or so the narrative goes.

Joseph Weizenbaum of MIT's Artificial Intelligence Laboratory and creator of the ELIZA program pioneered the chatbot revolution in the 1960s. Siri took the trend mainstream in 2011. Customer service and support departments quickly embraced the use of chatbots, mainly as a way to reduce service costs while being available to customers anytime, anywhere. The momentum continues, with Gartner predicting that more than 85 percent of customer interactions will be managed with zero human interaction by 2020.

Whether we realize it, most of us already interact with bots. Not long ago, we stopped at gas stations to ask for directions when we were lost, hoping the attendant knew north from south (and that you could remember what they said when you returned to your car). No more. Today we have GPS, Siri, Alexa, Waze, Google Assistant, Slack, Lyft, HealthTap, Hello Barbie, and a slew of messaging applications and intelligent bots to help guide us through our days.

Despite their usefulness, employees are increasingly fearful that AI and robots could put their own jobs in jeopardy. And rightly so. Industrial robots—those used in manufacturing—will have the biggest impact on jobs. Research from the National Bureau of Economic Research shows that between 1990 and 2007, when one or more industrial robots were introduced into the workforce, it led to the elimination of 6.2 jobs within a local area where people commute for work.

According to research by Forrester, *intelligent agents* powered by AI will destroy 6 percent of all jobs in the US by 2021, with the biggest effect felt in transportation, logistics, and customer service(s).[12] Similarly, a study by Oxford University suggests the top five jobs at risk of automation are loan officers, reception and information clerks, paralegals, retail salespeople, and taxi drivers and chauffeurs.

But what about marketing jobs? A separate study by Oxford University and Deloitte at the end of 2015 predicts that the risk is less pronounced specifically for marketers. For *marketing associate professionals*, it is fairly unlikely (33 percent) that their jobs will be automated over the next twenty years and for *marketing and sales directors*, it is very unlikely (1 percent). But that doesn't mean AI won't have a huge effect on the marketing and communications professions.

Gail Heimann, president of global communications firm Weber Shandwick, believes AI is rapidly transforming business and marketing processes. The firm conducted a survey that found 55 percent of CMOs expect AI to have a greater impact on marketing and communications than social media has ever had.[13] That's quite a profound finding given the impact social media has had on the marketing profession in the past ten years!

Repetitive and often monotonous marketing tasks will continue to become automated. Advancements in AI will increasingly expose the difficult and open-ended problems that marketing automation cannot solve on its own. As rudimentary activities become more and more automated, marketers will have additional time to hone our customer insights, agility, and creativity skills.

The Reality Is You Need Both

The increased focus on data analytics and technology doesn't mean creativity is no longer useful or necessary. To the contrary, creativity is oftentimes enhanced through technology. Creativity *and* data analytics are needed. In fact, they work best when used in tandem.

Consider Disney. Behind all the magic created in Disney Theme Parks are countless engineers, artists, and designers who create the experience enjoyed by millions of guests each year.[14] Disney calls them Imagineers, a combination of imagination and engineering, bridging the gap between science and fantasy to create a believable make-believe world. Building upon the legacy of Walt Disney, Imagineers bring art and science together to turn fantasy into reality and dreams into magic.

Burger King is another company that has unlocked the magic in data. Burger King global CMO Axel Schwan (and Cannes Lions Creative Marketer of the Year for 2017) believes stories are the connecting link between data and brilliant creative. Schwan says,

"I believe the more you know about your brand's target group, the better the creative work will be. Data is absolutely critical here. But then you need the best people in the world working for your brand to be able to find the relevant insights and stories in the data to develop an inspiring brief. The story coming out of the data is the connecting link to outstanding creative work."[15]

Whether it's melding science and fantasy or unearthing more powerful stories, data and creativity must learn to coexist in today's hypercompetitive-short-attention-span world. It's time for these two warring factions to cooperate instead of compete.

It's Time to Sharpen Our Creativity

When asked, half of all people will lament that they just aren't creative. And they're probably right—if you don't think you're creative, then you probably aren't. The good news, though, is that you *can* become more creative by changing your mindset. Anyone can innovate if they believe they can and if they practice.

Much has been written about how to foster creativity within your company, your team, and yourself. In addition to adopting an *I am creative* mindset, there are a number of no-cost things you can do on a daily basis to ignite your creative spark. They range from trying new things to practicing mental imagery, from asking more questions to reading more fiction, from practicing solitude to daydreaming.

Author and *New York Times* columnist Thomas Friedman believes in looking at everything with a new set of eyes. He tells the story of the advice he received as a greenhorn newspaper journalist: Take a different route to work each day. That way he wouldn't get caught up in the rut of routine and miss the stories that might have been happening around him.[16] By challenging the *we did that before* sentiment, you come up with different results and new approaches.

Larry Kim, founder and CTO of WordStream, published an infographic with nine ways to become more creative in the next ten minutes.[17] His suggestions include:

1. **Doodle something.** Doodling can help you stay present, engaged, and enhance recall.

2. **Sign up for a class in something you've never done before.** Creativity flourishes when you get out of your comfort zone.

3. **Create the right environment.** Make your environment a creative safe space where unusual ideas are celebrated.

4. **Pause the brainstorming and move your body.** Physically move your body while you consider a project from new angles.

5. **Start a sketchbook.** Draw for the enjoyment and reap benefits across your activities.

6. **Keep toys on your desk.** Building something physically with your hands can be just the creative jolt you need.

7. **Engage in flash fiction.** Try writing 100-word stories to get creative juices flowing.

8. **Try the thirty circles test.** Draw thirty circles, then turn each one into an object.

9. **Role play away.** Role playing with coworkers can generate brilliant solutions and revelations.

Sandra Stewart, principle at Thinkshift Communications, suggests using a mix of creative strategies to avoid turning brainstorming sessions into forced collaborations.[18] When developing messaging and brand positioning, Stewart's five favorite creative exercises include:

1. **The Take Away.** Strip down your thoughts to their bare essentials to focus on one or two simple benefits or features. This is the opposite of the kitchen-sink approach and allows you to really zero in.

2. **Word Trees.** As the name suggests, this brainstorming session builds out words or terms related to a broad concept. It also allows those vital few concepts to bubble up to the main branches.

3. **Oblique Strategies.** Used as a way to break through creative blocks, this strategy starts with a series of random prompts. Created by musician Brian Eno and artist Peter Schmidt, the written prompts are available through their app, website, or as a deck of cards.

4. **The 5 Whys.** Turn your problem into a *why* question, such as *Why isn't our brand resonating with millennials?* Then list your answers. Pick one of those answers and ask *why*. Continue until you reach your fifth *why*, and you should uncover a true motivation or audience insight.

5. **Blue Sky.** This method is the opposite of the ones above in that there are no constraints. What might we do, or create, in a world with no limits on time, money, and resources? From there, figure out what needs to change or happen to make your *what if* a reality.

If none of these strategies works for you, perhaps just commit to having more fun. For in the words of Albert Einstein, "Creativity is intelligence having fun."

Summary

As marketers compete for a dwindling supply of consumer attention, the importance of brands being found and heard becomes increasingly challenging and important. Nothing less than stellar marketing and exceptional offerings are required, along with clutter-busting creativity. That's why I call creativity *the splash* in the *Marketing Flexology* elixir.

Thus far, we've covered the core ingredients of *Marketing Flexology* and modern marketing success: insight + agility + creativity. We've also talked about why initiating change and continuous improvement initiatives are your best defense to avert a marketing shakeup. In the chapters that follow, we will shift to the mindset and toolset needed to compete in today's better-faster-cheaper-smarter world.

Chapter 6 Key Takeaways:

- An overreliance on data, analytics, and automation produces campaigns that are *technically correct* but creatively boring and ineffective. Don't overlook the value of creativity.

- Research shows that creativity impacts business results in terms of revenue growth, market share, and talent acquisition.

- The ability to ask smart questions, think creatively, and act strategically can't be replicated by big data or marketing automation technologies. As such, creativity is marketing's best career insurance.

- We are creative by choice, not by chance. Marketers must ignite and foster creativity within their companies, teams, and selves through daily practice.

- Marketers need to sharpen the skills that robots and AI can't (yet) replicate: empathy, emotional intelligence, human judgment, strategic thinking, and creativity.

Chapter 7

MARKETING FLEXOLOGY MINDSET

"Only changes in mindsets can extend the frontiers of the possible."
—*Winston Churchill*

In the last chapter, we added the finishing touch to our *Marketing Flexology* brew: a splash of creativity. With our libation now perfected by equal parts insight and agility, well shaken, and served with a splash, we're ready to replicate and scale our recipe. In the remaining chapters, we delve into the game-changing *Marketing Flexology* management framework. Step 1 is adopting a winner's mindset.

MINDSET	FOUNDATION	DIALS	TOOLS
Business-First	Purpose	People	Communications Brief
Five Traits	People	Programs	Messaging Framework
	Process	Budgets	Marketing Playbook
		Agencies	Executive Dashboard
			Project Management Office

Changing your mindset can be downright challenging. Even when presented the facts, the reasons, the rationale, and a vision for an improved future state, it can be difficult to sway one's point of view. Admittedly, conformity and maintaining the status quo are a powerful force that acts as an enemy to this meaningful change. A study by the *Harvard Business Review* found that organizations put tremendous pressure on employees to conform instead of challenging the status quo. In a survey of more than 2,000 US employees across a wide range of industries, nearly 49 percent agreed with the statement "I regularly feel pressure to conform in this organization." Additionally, more than half said that people in their organizations do not question the status quo.[1]

That's a problem. Although not all conformity is bad—I detail the essential principles and processes of great marketing organizations in Chapter 8—we need to strike the right balance between stability and agility. Adopting the right mindset is step one to outsmart change and future-proof your career.

A Business-First Mindset

Over the fourteen years that I was with the Hewlett-Packard Company, I served six CEOs and six CMOs. Each brought a unique perspective, set of strategies . . . and change. I acquired a keen view into how differently marketing leaders managed their organizations when I was tapped to lead several company-wide transformations.

I observed that the career *winners* in these upheavals all shared a common trait: a business-first mindset. The leaders who placed their companies and customers first—before their teams and before themselves—emerged from transformation relatively unscathed. The *me-first* leaders who put their own careers and team ahead of their companies and customers suffered the biggest upset to their budgets, their teams, their standing, and even their jobs.

It was Vyomesh "VJ" Joshi, then executive vice president of HP's imaging and printing group, who first introduced me to the business-first way of thinking. It had long been VJ's mantra and, upon hearing it, quickly became mine. From these experiences I learned that a business-first mindset is by far the most important trait of a dynamic marketing leader.

When faced with any business decision, three factors naturally come into play: the impact of that decision on my company, on my team, and on my career. Putting your company or customer first—before your team and before yourself—is the best way to future-proof your career. The rationale is quite simple: A successful career requires a solvent company. How can you succeed if your company fails?

A Mindset that Spans Generations

Before you shrug off *business first* as a baby-boomer corporate holdover mindset that doesn't apply to today's new generation of employees, let me share with you some perspective.

Gary Burnison, CEO of Korn Ferry, sees a troubling rise in me-first leadership across a number of sectors, including sports, government, and corporate, where egocentric heads are more dominant than selfless, service-oriented ones. He even has a name for this phenomenon: "me-dership."[2] Millennials have been characterized as being flighty job-hoppers, with a sense of entitlement and little company loyalty.[3] So it stands to reason that the thought of putting *business first* would likely be rejected by younger workers.

Millennial attorney James Goodnow, coauthor of *Motivating Millennials*, disputes that view. "Many baby boomer executives think millennials are just cashing in on a short-term gig so they can scrape together enough money to go hike Mount Kilimanjaro or buy an unlimited annual skydiving pass. Millennials want stability—yes, that may shock you, but it's true."

As for job stability, the Bureau of Labor Statistics[4] reports that baby boomers job-hopped in their twenties just as frequently as millennials do now.

I am also reminded that my generation—the baby boomers—was also once referred to as the *me generation*. Joel Stein, an author and journalist who wrote for the *Los Angeles Times* and is a regular contributor to *TIME* magazine, compares the two: "Millennials' self-involvement is more a continuation of a trend than a revolutionary break from previous generations. They're not a new species; they've just mutated to adapt to their environment."

Millennials *are* the new baby boomers. According to Pew Research, in 2015 millennials became the largest generation in the US labor force, at 34 percent. And it's predicted that by 2024, three-quarters of workers globally will be millennials.

Indeed, a business-first mindset spans generations of employees. It has worked in the past; it will work for you now. If you want to outsmart change and future-proof your career and your team, a business-first mindset is your best protection.

Business First in Action

Let's look at a business-first mindset in action. Say your company is experiencing a challenging quarter caused by the arrival of an upstart competitor with an aggressive pricing strategy aimed at stealing market share. The CEO asks all business groups and functions to reduce any *nonessential spending and hiring* for the next few quarters to align with a declining sales forecast. As the marketing leader, you have three choices:

1. **My Career:** I could cut some marketing programs that I know aren't delivering up to par but, heck, let someone else step up to the challenge. Marketing is already way underbudgeted. If I give up budget dollars now, I'll never get them back. I'll respond that all planned marketing is

essential and already committed through the remainder of the calendar year. In fact, all planned marketing programs are designed to thwart this aggressive competitor from stealing away our customers. Yes, that sounds good.

2. **My Team:** I have a few open roles on the team that I could cancel. I could have an agency or a few contractors pick up the workload, but I don't want to lose any head count. I'll report that all planned new hires are *essential* and *already in the works* with offers extended. I better fill those open job requisitions now before there's an official hiring freeze.

3. **My Company:** My company is in a bind and, as a business leader, I am accountable. I will present my CEO with three budget-reducing alternatives, along with a trade-off analysis for each in terms of sales potential. I will additionally present some incremental customer-retention programs to safeguard our current installed base from this new competitive advance.

Marketers can get very clever when faced with an imminent budget and staff reduction. I've seen marketers reclassify their employees out of marketing job families and into sales or sales operations to hide their head count. I've witnessed managers lock in agency retainers to preserve their workforce levels. I've experienced marketing leaders commit to multiyear sponsorships to protect their budgets (and gain favor with the sponsoring organizations). I've seen managers terminate employees on a Friday, only to have them reappear Monday morning doing their exact same job as a contractor. The games people play!

What happens when we make business decisions based on the best interest of our team or our own career? We end up making decisions that maintain the status quo and preserve our budgets, our head count, our favorite programs, and our jobs. That may work in the short term but, over time, it weakens our company's financial health.

Asking yourself—is this in the best interest of my business—will help contribute to your company's fiscal health which, in turn, will ultimately be good for your team and for your own career.

Characteristics of a Business-First Leader

During my many marketing transformations, a business-first mindset was far and away the key differentiator between the career *winners* and the career *losers*. But there were also a number of other characteristics I observed. The winning marketing leaders kept things crisp and current. They built an organization that could pivot quickly with any business fluctuation. They kept their teams lean and used agency partners to absorb workload fluctuations. They focused on the outcome of their marketing activities, not just on the efficiency of their output. They focused not only on turning the crank, but also on moving the needle. They didn't dodge bullets, go under the radar, or fend off change; rather, they bucked up and held themselves accountable. They viewed themselves, and their teams, as an investment center for their companies. They took personal responsibility for every marketing dollar and asset with which they were entrusted. They believed that learning agility was a critical predictor of leadership success and were expert, lifelong learners. And, as a result, they were winners.

Let's take a closer look at the five key traits of a business-first leader along with examples of companies that exemplify these characteristics.

Trait 1: Nimble

A nimble leader is dexterous in movement and thought. As such, they can absorb and bounce back from unplanned change without slowing down. Internet entertainment services leader, Netflix Inc., is an example of a company that repeatedly exhibits its ability to adapt to changing technology and tastes, developing award-winning programming with a cultlike following.

Netflix originally launched in 1997 as a website that rented DVDs through mail posting and a traditional pay-per-rental model, competing with traditional retail rental models such as Blockbuster and Hollywood Video. In the early 2000s, Netflix dropped this model and launched its now well-known subscription model. In 2007, the company introduced video on demand, allowing Internet users to watch content directly from their devices.[5] When many companies faltered in 2009, the peak of the recession, Netflix gained three million members due to their new TV and movie streaming plan, which allowed subscribers to stream an unlimited amount of entertainment a month, along with their disc-delivery service. As of 2017, Netflix continued to grow with over 109 million members in more than 190 countries enjoying more than 125 million hours of TV shows and movies per day—all without commercials or commitments.[6]

Trait 2: Lean

Keeping their operations and teams lean is the second trait of a business-first leader. These enlightened leaders know that bloated organizations can quickly become sluggish, zap agility, and become an easy target during belt-tightening times. It is hard to find a leaner marketing organization than Tesla Inc.

Tesla is breaking all the rules of automotive marketing. Whereas in 2016 rival Nissan spent $4.3 million advertising its electric Nissan Leaf, Tesla spent zero. The company has no advertising, no ad agency, no CMO, and no dealer network. And that doesn't appear to be a problem.[7] Tesla has built a strong brand that requires little or no promotion for now, relying instead on word-of-mouth, passionate advocates, and free media coverage thanks to a CEO who understands the power of showmanship. That seems to be enough to fuel demand for the foreseeable future. At the time of this writing, Tesla has more orders than they can build—that in itself is great marketing.[8]

Trait 3: Effective

One of the characteristics that distinguish a leader from a manager is a focus on the effectiveness of their marketing strategy rather than purely on the efficiency of various marketing tactics. A business-first leader places outcomes ahead of outputs. As famed author and management consultant Peter Drucker said, "Management is doing things right; leadership is doing the right things." Medjet Assist is an example of a company that believes *less is more* and has results to prove it.

The marketing team at Medjet Assist, the air medical transport and travel protection company, was good at generating a steady stream of sales leads. The company's sales team, unfortunately, was investing valuable time and energy following up on leads that weren't qualified. Bill Miller, chief sales and marketing officer at Medjet Assist, knew something had to change. "By taking the time to understand our target audience and testing different call-to-action messages, we honed our lead generation to focus on those most likely to convert. The result: more qualified leads and more sales. Less is more!" says Miller.[9]

Trait 4: Accountable

Accountability is the fourth trait of a business-first leader. There's more to accountability than simply measuring and reporting on the results of your marketing campaigns. The accountable leader looks at the impact their total marketing investment has on driving value, profit, and financial return on investment. That often requires the CMO and CFO working together, like they do at Revlon.

When Lorenzo Delpani took over as Revlon CEO in 2014, he established a guiding framework, called the Strategy for Value Creation, for the entire company. The framework ensures that every member of the Revlon organization—including agencies and outside partners—knows how to contribute value to the company. Benjamin Karsch, EVP and chief marketing officer of Revlon Consumer, says the strategy identifies the levers employees need to pull across the whole company to create shareholder value. "Many of those levers impact on things marketing does every day, such as price optimization, shift of brand support to highest ROI investments, and development of fewer, bigger, better new product innovations. We train our people on how to pull those levers; the financial impact that it has when you do pull them; and the mathematical formula to drive enterprise value creation from pulling those levers." This approach requires genuine collaboration between finance and marketing.

As Karsch explains: "The role of the CFO is to guide on the financial impact of the decisions that we're making. But the CFO cannot be successful as a police officer against marketers. Marketers also need to be trained and focused on the right thing."[10]

Marketers who can demonstrate their impact on the top and bottom line will be well positioned to make the business case for ongoing investment. What smart CFO wouldn't choose to reallocate budget to those initiatives driving the highest and most predictable shareholder value across the company?

Trait 5: Learning

A commitment to continuously grow and learn is the final trait of a business-first leader. While the majority of learning comes through on-the-job experience, mentoring, and coaching, a percentage also comes from self-initiated training, courses, and reading. The learning and development community have a name for this framework: the *70:20:10 model*. The majority of learning—70 percent—is through doing; 20 percent of learning is from trusted colleagues and mentors; and 10 percent is through more formal classroom courses, webinars, seminars, etcetera, with formal assessments.[11] The model continues to be widely employed, and adapted, by organizations throughout the world, including The Coca-Cola Company.

Coke has embraced the 70:20:10 ratio, innovatively applying it to their digital marketing. The framework guides the company's content development and investment by dividing it into "now, new and next." Seventy percent of Coke's digital marketing budget is devoted to bread-and-butter marketing efforts, or what it calls "now"; 20 percent is allocated to what it deems is "new," to innovating on the things that worked in the 70 percent category; and 10 percent is allocated to what it calls "next," or ideas that are completely untested.[12] The 70 percent programs are low risk, not overly time consuming, and most importantly, pay the bills. The 20 percent lays the groundwork for the future and helps Coke outpace the competition. These are emerging areas that are starting to gain traction and represent safe learning opportunities. The 10 percent is focused on high-risk, high-reward programs—groundbreaking ideas that haven't been tested before but can pay big future dividends.

As marketers, there is much we can learn from and emulate: Netflix's nimbleness that keeps it out front of technology trends and consumer tastes; Tesla's lean mentality that has amassed it a huge loyal following without spending money on traditional marketing; Medjet Assist's focus on effectiveness by adopting a *less is more* strategy; Revlon's focus on accountability, partnering with finance to deliver strategic value to the company; and Coke's commitment to learning by focusing 30 percent of its digital marketing budget on innovation, testing, and learning. Taken together, these five traits, and a business-first mindset, form the foundation of the *Marketing Flexology* management framework.

Summary

The disciplined and enlightened marketing leader knows that they and their teams must be nimble, lean, effective, accountable, and learning. Above all, today's modern marketing leader possesses a *business-first* mindset, putting the needs of his company or customer before the needs of his team or himself.

Armed with a business-first mindset, we are now ready to tackle the *Marketing Flexology* toolset (foundation, dials, tools). The remaining chapters of this book will show you exactly how to apply these five traits and this mindset in the day-to-day management of your teams, budgets, agencies, and marketing programs.

Chapter 7 Key Takeaways:

- When making any business decision, do what's right for your company (or customer) first, then for your team, and last for yourself. You will never go wrong.

- A successful career needs a solvent company. You can't win if your company loses.

- Put some skin in the game by adopting a *business-first* mindset . . . and watch the career magic happen.

- Millennials *are* the new boomers: A *Marketing Flexology* mindset is as relevant and critical to today's marketing leaders as it was before.

- A business-first leader is *nimble, lean, effective, accountable,* and *learning.* These five traits distinguish the career *winners* from the *losers* in a marketing transformation.

Chapter 8

MARKETING FLEXOLOGY FOUNDATION

"You can't build a great building on a weak foundation. You must have a solid foundation if you're going to have a strong superstructure."
—*Gordon B. Hinckley*

In Chapter 7, we took the first step in our marketing agility journey. Step 1 includes honing five traits (*nimble, lean, effective, accountable*, and *learning*) and embracing a business-first mindset. In this chapter, we take the next step: laying the foundation of the *Marketing Flexology* management framework. A strong marketing foundation allows marketing teams to operate more intelligently, efficiently, and productively. It ensures everyone has a common understanding of how things work or should work. The foundation also serves as the strong and flexible backbone for the steps to follow—the *Marketing Flexology* dials and tools— so it is critical we set it right.

The *Marketing Flexology* foundation is comprised of three core elements: *purpose, people*, and *process*. A well-defined charter and agreed-to support model allows marketing teams to confidentially move forward with clear *purpose*. Having clear strategies in place for deploying *people*, yields maximum productivity and value from your marketing talent. A well-defined marketing *process* will enable your marketers to do their very best work without confusion or delay.

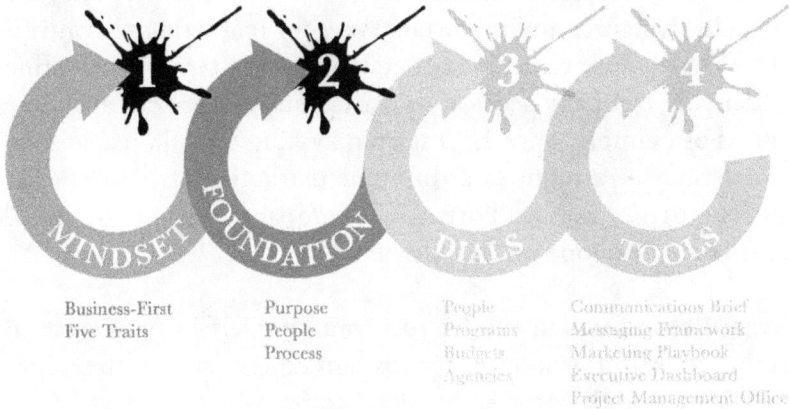

MINDSET	**FOUNDATION**	**DIALS**	**TOOLS**
Business-First	Purpose	People	Communications Brief
Five Traits	People	Programs	Messaging Framework
	Process	Budgets	Marketing Playbook
		Agencies	Executive Dashboard
			Project Management Office

Together, purpose, people, and process form a strong and resilient marketing foundation that can withstand any management change or business fluctuation. Let's look at how to shape and develop each of them in greater detail.

PURPOSE: Get Crystal-Clear on Charter

Marketing teams come in all shapes and sizes. Some are tactical, others strategic. Some are product focused, others customer focused. Some lead with creativity, others with data and analytics. Though there are countless permutations, marketing organizations tend to organize in one of three general structures.

1. The first type of organization operates as a *marketing service provider*, serving as an in-house marketing agency for the company.

2. The second type of marketing organization functions as a *marketing advisor* to the CEO and executive team, primarily on brand and reputation matters.

3. The third marketing organization operates as a business partner and *driver of new growth*.

I'm not advocating one marketing model over another. They are all valid structures and important ways for marketing to contribute. What's more critical is understanding the type of marketing leader your company needs at its current stage of growth and revenue.[1] For example, a pre-IPO startup looking to build recognition and create buzz requires a different marketing structure—and leader—than a mature Fortune 50 company striving for global consistency and operational efficiency.

Regardless of which model you find yourself in or choose to build, it is important to secure agreement across the organization . . . and not just by the person who wrote your job description. Ideally, we have buy-in on marketing's mission and role from across the entire executive team. This includes business unit heads, regional teams, and functional leaders. At a minimum, we need strong advocacy from the chairman, CEO, or president—preferably all three—as this triumvirate typically consults on all C-level hirings and firings.

To be clear, advocacy does not give us a hall pass. We must earn our titles each and every day by delivering excellent marketing. Support, collaboration, and respect follow as a result. It's not the other way around.

Let's look at the characteristics of each of the three operating models.

Model 1: Marketing Service Provider

In the service provider model, the key priority is efficiency— building a set of shared services that can be leveraged across our company, providing greater cost effectiveness for all.

That is typically accomplished by consolidating around a small set of approved suppliers and a core set of marketing tools or platforms that are broadly deployed. These might include campaign planning and reporting, lead nurturing and pipeline management, translation services, content management, and the like.

A heavy focus on administration, operations, policies, and councils drives global alignment in this model. Additionally, internal client satisfaction—how happy we keep our inside stakeholders—is a key measure of our success . . . and longevity. Let's take a look at a company where marketing is structured as a global marketing service provider.

In September 2016, Unilever made headlines by announcing a significant centralization of its global and local marketing functions into a single team. The move aims to ensure its marketers are better equipped in today's "super-connected" consumer landscape. As part of the move, local marketing teams would report to global marketing teams, rather than to local general managers.[2]

The move to a centralized global marketing structure is part of Unilever's plan to double efficiency savings from its brand and marketing investment by 2019. But it's more than just a cost-cutting drive. By telling a more consistent brand story, Unilever also aims to bolster its marketing effectiveness. As part of that drive, the company is cutting the number of ads it creates by 30 percent and plans to consolidate the number of creative agencies it works with by half.[3] For Unilever, moving to a centralized service provider model is what's needed to successfully market in today's connected world.

Model 2: Marketing Advisor

In the marketing advisor model, the key priority is enhancing a company's brand and reputation. We often see this model in a distributed marketing organization where there is a distinction between *corporate marketing* and *business unit marketing*, with the latter's emphasis on demand generation. Functional leadership is largely dispersed in this model, with each business unit having its own finance, IT, HR, and marketing leaders.

In this model, the CMO has strategic leadership and title, but not the end-to-end direct authority. The corporate team in this model manages and enforces the company's core brand, identity assets, and standards. Additionally, the corporate team drives those initiatives involving the executive team, including customer advisory councils, large customer events, key sponsorships, signature communiques, and global branding campaigns. These are called C-level touches. As such, the CEO, president, or chairman often decides priorities and alignment in this model. McDonald's is a brand that has successfully managed the delicate balance between global direction and distributed execution.

While keeping its overarching branding consistent, McDonald's practices "glocal" marketing efforts. The approach provides global strategic direction along with the flexibility to adapt to local opportunities and requirements. Region and country marketing teams have wide latitude to meet the needs of their local markets within a global strategic framework. That's why McDonald's can introduce macarons to its French menu, McArabia, a flatbread sandwich, to its restaurants in the Middle East, and the McItaly burger to its menu in Italy, accompanied by local marketing. This "glocal" approach helped put McDonald's at #9 on *Interbrand's Best Global Brands 2014*. (It ranks #12 on the 2017 listing.)[4] McDonald's ability to cater to local tastes, customs, and consumer needs has made the company the world's leading global food service retailer.

Model 3: Business Growth Driver

In the third operating model, marketing is viewed as a business leader and driver of growth, partnering across the executive team to drive the corporate growth agenda. In this structure, marketing drives end-to-end alignment across product, region, and corporate strategies, and develops marketing initiatives that result in higher revenues and margins for the company.

In the driver of growth model, a shared partnership with the executive team is critical to success. In some organizations, marketing may even have accountability for its own P&L, placing marketing on an equal footing with other revenue-generating business units. Such is the case at the Eastman Kodak Company.

Steven Overman is the global CMO of Kodak, and the president of their consumer and film division. Overman is leading a companywide renewal of the Kodak brand to increase its power, relevance, and value. By leading the consumer-facing division, he also controls the business levers to grow the value of the brand.[5] Says Overman: "Not only do I work closely with our CEO on our business objectives, I also continually collaborate with our chief financial officer, chief HR officer, chief technology officer, and chief legal counsel. Meanwhile, as a business division president, I also walk in the shoes of a P&L owner, which enables me to truly understand the broad requirements of effective business leadership. I would encourage every marketing executive to lean into broader business responsibilities." Although Kodak's dual-hatted CMO is not a widely prevalent model, it is certainly one of the most advantageous for a marketing leader.

Regardless of Model, Three Lessons I Learned

Over my marketing career, I've worked in each of these three marketing models. They all have their pluses and minuses along with their challenges and rewards. Regardless of the marketing model you find yourself in, there are three important things to remember.

1. Have a clearly defined mission and scope. Spell out what's in the charter and what's out of charter—this is especially important if you are working with limited resources (which nowadays is always the case).

2. Secure advocacy for your operating model from across the leadership team, including business unit heads,

regional teams, and functional leaders. Of course, this is in addition to the advocacy from the chairman, CEO, and president.

3. Deliver each and every day. I've found that the best way to gain cooperation and support is to outperform and overdeliver on expectations—not only internally, but out in the marketplace where it really matters.

PEOPLE: Only the RIGHT People Are Our Greatest Asset

People are the second cornerstone of the *Marketing Flexology* management framework. We've all heard the saying "People are our greatest asset." Overused and somewhat trite, the sentiment finds its way into messages from the chairman, HR communiques, annual reports, and even taglines. When research firm Gallup proclaims that 68 percent of the US workplace is either "not engaged" or "actively disengaged,"[6] it's hard to believe this platitude. In fact, some might say that people are our greatest liability.

In his LinkedIn post, Bill Nash argues, "Only the right people are our greatest asset."[7] Nash believes attitude should be as important to the hiring decision as experience, knowledge, and skills, but is often neglected. Julie Weber, vice president of People for Southwest Airlines, echoes Nash's sentiment. She credits the airline's success to "hiring the right people, at the right time, with the right attitude."

Placing a higher emphasis and value on an employee's mindset—some call these "soft skills"—makes sense. But that doesn't diminish the need for a workforce with the right mix of experience and skills. As companies grow, shrink, expand, morph, and mature, the talent they need changes as well. That's why investors often replace founders of startups with *experienced talent* to achieve the next stage of growth.

The team you assembled to launch your idea ten years ago is different than what you need today to lead your company through a transformation, merger, or acquisition. The skillset you needed as a young regional startup is different than what you need today as you establish yourself as a national or even global player. Not only do you need the right people at the right time to keep pace with your changing business, but you also need the right kind of marketers to keep up with customers who are changing faster than those same marketers.

John Ellett, author of *The CMO Manifesto* and contributor to the *Forbes* CMO Network, says that customer expectations are changing faster than marketers' abilities to keep up. While tools are evolving to better manage customer experiences, recent research shows the skills and organizational processes needed at most companies, unfortunately, are still lacking.[8] A Forrester Research study commissioned by Oracle[9] indicates the adoption of modern marketing capabilities is lagging, with only 11 percent of respondents identified as "modern marketers" and most as "experienced" marketers (33 percent), "discovery" marketers (41 percent), or "novice" marketers (15 percent).

Talent: Make or Buy?

In an ideal world, we would:

- Proactively attract new marketing talent to fill our talent pipeline
- Have a well-documented career progression framework and process in place
- Conduct disciplined (and sincere) succession planning
- Deploy talent management strategies to reward, recognize, and motivate marketing talent in our organizations

- Develop strong relationships with local and leading universities to seed new talent through internships and entry-level roles

In an ideal world, we would be ready to fill any new need or opening at a moment's notice. As you can imagine, that doesn't always work out. We need to add an SEO/SEM whiz, for instance, and don't have the talent in house. We need to build a social media or content team and find we haven't had the time to cultivate that skill internally. As a result, we often need to fill an immediate vacancy NOW and turn to outside readymade talent because we haven't developed from within. *We buy expertise because it's more expedient.*

It happens at the highest levels of a company all the time. The top job (CEO) is increasingly going to outsiders when boards have time to plan for succession, which was the case for nearly three-quarters of CEO hires from 2012 to 2015.[10] Why should filling marketing positions be any different? It doesn't have to be this way. It's a negative trend that can be reversed if you have the right people strategies in place.

People Strategies that Work

Here are three strategies I have applied to marketing talent over the years with good results:

1. Design First, Staff Second

How big of a marketing staff do you need? Probably not as large as you think, but it does depend on which of the three *marketing models* you operate in and the work that needs to be accomplished. Unilever's move to a centralized global model, for example, clearly requires less marketing head count, budget, and agency partners than did its previous decentralized model. McDonald's "glocal" strategy, on the other hand, likely results in more total marketing resources to support each of the 119 countries in which it operates. Kodak's joint CMO and business P&L owner model likely drives large economies of scale by eliminating redundant resources while improving time to market. Once you clearly define the work outcomes, you can then begin to design a marketing organization that is affordable, appropriately sized, correctly scoped in terms of job levels and titles and, only then, staffed with the very best talent.

Sounds logical, right? But too often marketing leaders go about it backwards. They design an organization around their existing people (or friends they want to recruit). Or, worse, they put the wrong people in the wrong roles. Ron Carucci, cofounder and managing partner at Navalent, said it well: "Jobs, like organizations, must be carefully crafted not around people's preferences or idiosyncrasies, but around needed work and outcomes."[11]

I've known VPs with no direct reports, directors who reported to directors, and even managers with a one-person staff. I've seen directors promoted to senior director without any change to their job responsibilities. I've witnessed managers promoted to directors with no change in pay. I've worked with individuals holding the title of VP of marketing strategy who have never written, or executed, a marketing strategy in their life. In each of these instances, the boss accommodated her people rather than focusing on the work that needed to get done.

Why do leaders do this? Sometimes to appease; other times as gratitude or payback; often because they are afraid they might lose the employee; and sometimes because it's easier to *give them what they want* than to be objective and honest. This is another reason why cultivating a business-first mindset is so important, as covered in Chapter 7.

Whatever the reason, each of these examples sends a signal to the rest of your organization that it's not about merit or qualifications, but rather how you play the game. A former Hewlett-Packard CEO used to say, "Every promotion and demotion sends a signal to the organization about what you value." It certainly does.

2. Staff for the Valley, Not for the Peak

As you'll recall from Chapter 7, staying *nimble* and *lean* are two of the core traits of a *Marketing Flexology* mindset. This outlook is really put to the test when staffing our marketing organizations.

Marketers are known for being an optimistic lot.[12] We're convinced we will gain traction faster, win more frequently, grow demand more steadily, and achieve forecasts more easily than we actually do. As a result, we often staff for the *best of times*. When building a marketing organization, however, it might be better to be a pessimist and staff for the *worst of times*.

It is very painful when the message comes down that your department needs to reduce head count. Frankly, it's just a matter of time. Every week we read headlines such as:

> *Another round of layoffs*
> *Workforce reductions coming*
> *Permanent staff made redundant*
> *Positions being eliminated*
> *Job cuts planned*

Marketing layoffs are less likely to happen when we staff for the valley, not for the peak. When you staff for the valley, you may have unexpected high demand times with crushing workloads, but you also are better able to weather any downturn in business. To handle the peak workload demands, you will need to develop a network of trusted individuals and agency partners you can turn to.

3. Know When to Outsource

The third people strategy is outsourcing excess marketing demand. There are a number of good reasons to bolster internal talent with external individuals or agencies. They can extend our reach, provide a specialized skill we don't have in-house, provide an outsourced service at a lower cost, or provide fortification during peak periods when we need more hands on deck.

The outsourcing decision usually boils down to the following questions: When is the right time to outsource your marketing workload, and how do you chose the right resource? Jayson DeMers, contributor to *Forbes*, identifies seven warning signs that signal it's time to start outsourcing your marketing:[13]

1. Your revenue isn't growing fast enough.

2. Your marketing staff is overworked.

3. You always seem to be running behind.

4. Your marketing strategies are thrown together.

5. You're limited to a handful of channels.

6. You focus too much on tasks and not enough on strategy.

7. You're disappointed with your marketing results.

The challenge then becomes making sure you have the right external resources in place to manage a marketing avalanche. When engaging with outside talent, there are always concerns about quality, turnaround time, privacy, and cost. Typically, hiring a *bona fide* agency is more expensive than having your in-house team develop marketing materials. But tapping into a flexible workforce could save you money if done strategically.

According to the US Bureau of Labor Statistics[14], salaries usually account for nearly 70 percent of an employee's total compensation package. The remaining 30 percent goes to taxes and benefits. Realistically, you have an opportunity to save 30 percent when using outsourced marketing resources. In addition, you pay only for what you need.

Knowing when and how to outsource allows you to stay nimble and lean without adding to your fixed head count costs. Yes, it will take some added guiding, directing, and training on your part, but it can certainly lighten the marketing workload and help avoid painful downsizings.

PROCESS: Marketers Hate Process

Process is the third guiding principle of the *Marketing Flexology* management framework. Talk to any marketer about process, governance, or compliance, and watch their eyes glaze over. Many professionals find marketing processes punishing, restrictive, and limiting to their creative freedom.

There's really no escaping marketing process, even in the wild west of social media marketing. Even tweets now require businesses to establish an internal process and oversight to avoid Federal Trade Commission (FTC) violations. This policy was established after Sony and its advertising agency misled consumers with deceptive Twitter endorsements.[15]

Can you imagine if there were no *rules of the road* for drivers? It would be complete chaos. Same holds true for marketing organizations without process—it can be quite disastrous.

The larger and more geographically dispersed the marketing organization, the greater the need for processes. And that's not all bad. Processes can help unify your brand, drive cost savings, ensure consistency in message, maintain high quality standards, increase efficiency, and more. The trick is to put processes in place that *work for you,* rather than processes that *you work for.*

There are really only six core marketing processes that you need, at least initially. You need a lightweight process to help you *coordinate* marketing activities, to quickly *allocate* marketing resources, to efficiently *orchestrate* your outbound activities, to *calculate* the effect of your marketing programs, to help you *remediate* any exceptions or disagreements that might occur, and a process to help you *celebrate* wins, milestones, and accomplishments.

The Six Core Marketing Processes

To keep it simple, start with a handful of key marketing processes. You can download a process flowchart for each of these six core processes from my website, www.marketingflexology.com.

1. **Planning:** How and when strategic and tactical marketing plans are proposed and finalized

2. **Budgeting:** How and when budgets and other resources are decided and allocated

3. **Customer Engagement:** A consolidated view and calendar of planned customer interactions and outreach for the upcoming year

4. **Measurement:** How and when programs will be tracked, measured, and reported on

5. **Exception and Escalations:** How disagreements and needed exceptions get resolved

6. **Next Practices:** How institutional knowledge, experiences, and achievements are shared, leveraged, and celebrated

Admittedly, establishing a process is more than just a handsome flowchart documenting the how-to steps. It often means putting the right tools and technologies in place to support each process—usually a backend database and a frontend user interface.

It also requires a disciplined marketing leader who reinforces the importance of the *rules of the road* on a consistent basis. However, I can guarantee you that these six core processes will make your marketing smarter, your team more productive, and your organization more effective.

Summary

Regardless of whether you are building a team, inheriting one, dismantling, transforming, or right-sizing, all marketing organizations benefit from having a solid marketing foundation at their core. This consists of a well-defined charter and operating model, clear and meaningful roles and strategies for deploying people, and a set of lightweight processes that enable a smooth and steady flow of brilliant marketing work. These guiding elements should be documented, discussed, and internalized by every member of the team. Without this foundation, a marketing organization can quickly become bloated, misaligned, unaccountable, and unproductive—the opposite of a *Marketing Flexology* organization.

With a strong foundation, you can weather most business fluctuations. And that's a very good way to outsmart change and future-proof your marketing, your team, and your career. This Malay proverb captures it well: "A tree with strong roots laughs at storms."

Chapter 8 Key Takeaways:

- The #1 reason CMOs fail is not a lack of performance, it is a lack of role clarity. Get crystal-clear on your charter.

- Design first, staff second—not the other way around.

- Using outside resources to supplement your internal team is a calculated risk worth taking.

- Keep your marketing processes lightweight, flexible, and simple. A great process provides clear guidelines within which marketers can do their best work.

- Any marketing process you adopt should help you better coordinate, allocate, orchestrate, calculate, remediate, and celebrate your marketing success. If it doesn't, ditch it.

Chapter 9

MARKETING FLEXOLOGY DIALS

"Incredible change happens in your life when you decide to take control of what you have power over instead of craving control over what you don't."
—*Steve Maraboli*

In Chapter 8, we took the second step in our marketing agility journey by laying a strong organizational foundation able to withstand the forceful and often chaotic winds of change. With a clearly defined purpose and operating model, the right people in the right roles, and a process that drives efficiency and speed, we have a solid foundation for the next steps on our road to marketing agility. Next, we'll cover Step 3 in the *Marketing Flexology* management framework: the *Marketing Flexology dials*. Unlike the winds of change, these four dials are 100 percent within our control.

They include:

1. People

2. Programs

3. Budgets

4. Agencies

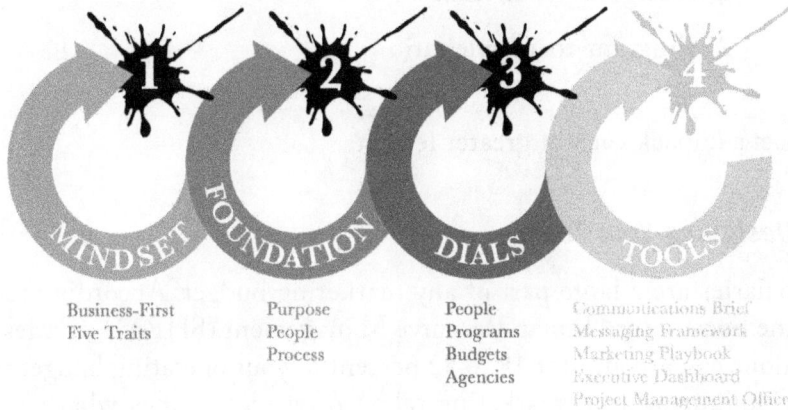

Business-First	Purpose	People	Communications Brief
Five Traits	People	Programs	Messaging Framework
	Process	Budgets	Marketing Playbook
		Agencies	Executive Dashboard
			Project Management Office

In this chapter, we'll explore ways to fine-tune these four dials to achieve optimum performance and avert a major career blowout. With a firm hand on the controls, marketing leaders can quickly dial up or down when faced with changing business dynamics and direction. This gives us immense marketing agility—the ability to seize an opportunity and turn it into an *Oreo moment*.[1]

To achieve this level of marketing agility, we must first minimize our fixed costs and maximize our variable costs. You'll see this theme repeated throughout each of the sections that follow.

Turning the Dial on PEOPLE

In the early days of marketing, there were only a handful of choices when staffing your organization. Those included: full time or part time, salaried or hourly, exempt or nonexempt, and permanent or temporary. Today's marketing leaders have far more creative options in sourcing, hiring, and designing their teams.

There are many aspects to managing and optimizing your people resources. We'll cover two in this section:

1. Designing your team

2. Program-to-people ratio

Let's unpack each at greater length.

Designing Your Team

Salaries are a large part of any marketing budget. According to the Society for Human Resource Management (SHRM), salaries alone can account for 18 to 52 percent of your operating budget.[2] Configuring your marketing talent often determines what you have left to run your marketing campaigns.

Traditional employment models were pretty unimaginative and limiting. Employees once prized *permanent full-time* positions because they provided stability and job security. But that is no longer the case. The implicit contract between employee and employer is long dead, and even full-time employment is *at will*.

Today there's a whole cadre of nontraditional employment options and work arrangements that provide employees greater job flexibility and employers greater budget control.

The nonemployee workforce—often referred to as the *gig economy*, the *flex economy* or, *on-demand labor*—is on the rise. Freelancers now make up 35 percent of US workers.[3] That number is expected to balloon to 50 percent by 2020.

Even in the executive ranks, we are seeing some creative hiring practices. Take for instance the fractional, interim, or outsourced CMO.[4] Unlike a full-time executive, these hybrid CMOs often work part time, off site, or for a short duration. They are brought in when the business can't afford a full-time CMO but needs to kickstart an initiative such as a rebrand or digital transformation. Typically, hybrid CMOs are less expensive than hiring a large management consultancy.[5]

This trend toward a more flexible workforce is expected to grow. According to Deloitte's 2016 Global Human Capital Trends study, 51 percent of global executives say their organizations plan to increase the use of flexible and independent workers in the next three to five years.[6] Staffing your marketing team with a blend of full-time and flexible workers will help minimize your fixed costs and maximize your variable costs. That translates to more resources available to fuel demand-driving programs.

Program-to-People Ratios

Doing more with less has long been a mantra in the business world, and marketing is no exception. The program-to-people ratio compares the ratio of program expense to staff expense in the marketing budget. The goal is to have fewer people running more programs, hitting a high ratio such as 60:40 or even 70:30.

Of course, some programs and functions are more budget intensive and others more labor intensive. One marketer might be able to run a dozen ad campaigns, but it may take a dozen marketers to run a single C-level event. A blended program-to-people average across your entire marketing organization is what you should look at.

You can raise (improve) the ratio by strategically outsourcing key marketing activities to freelancers or agencies since it transfers people dollars to program dollars. This might be a better alternative than hiring additional internal staff. A good rule of thumb is to feel a pinch but avoid the temptation of adding more staff. This is what's meant by "staff for the valley, not for the peak," covered in Chapter 8.

Here are some considerations for managing the people dial that can help minimize fixed costs and maximize your overall flexibility:

1. **Understand your fully burdened labor rate.** The true cost of an employee is much higher than his or her base salary. You need to factor in the additional cost to your

company—and to your budget—to cover employment taxes, benefits, space, equipment, recruiting expenses, training, and other costs. This could easily add 30 percent or more to the salaries you pay to employees. Stated another way, these expenses will take a bite out of the total *people budget* you have to work with and need to be factored into your plans. Finance and HR can guide you here.

2. **Determine your optimal program-to-people ratio.** As a starting point, aim to allocate 70 percent of your total marketing envelope to programs and 30 percent to people. The more dollars you focus on customer-facing in-market activities versus internal staff costs, the most impactful your overall marketing organization becomes. For example, if your total marketing budget is $10 million, try earmarking $7 million for *programs* with the remaining $3 million allocated for *people*. Keep in mind the $3 million for people is really $2.1 million (or less) in actual base salaries once you account for taxes and benefits. That reduced amount will cover an approximate twelve- to fifteen-person in-house team (USD).

3. **Decide your priority in-house roles.** Depending on your industry, there will be certain core competencies you will want to develop and grow internally; you can outsource the remaining roles to your flexible workforce or agency partners. For example, if you're a B2B marketer, business relationships might be your main focus. In-house skills you'll need include product marketing, partner marketing, campaign development, event management, sales enablement, and lead management, among others. On the other hand, if you're a B2C marketer, your focus is brand recognition, customer transactions, and experiences. You'll need in-house expertise in consumer insight, brand positioning, creative development, social media marketing, online commerce, and web analytics, among others. Admittedly these are broad generalizations, but they serve as a good starting point.

Turning the Dial on PROGRAMS

Programs are the second dial within marketing's control. Programs are activities that help you achieve your marketing objectives. They are the face of the company to its customers and the lifeblood of any marketing organization. They are also how marketing budgets get allocated and marketing departments get graded, so programs receive a lot of attention.

Sometimes a program's goal is to get someone to take immediate action that moves him or her closer to purchase. This is referred to as *demand marketing*. Other times a program's goal is to build a favorable perception and trusting reputation over an extended period. This is referred to as *brand marketing*.

In many companies, separate individuals or teams drive brand management and demand generation. A corporate marketing team usually leads brand; a business, product, or region team typically leads demand. That often results in some internal arm wrestling, especially when budgets are tight or being squeezed.

While tension between the two can be healthy, the reality is it's not an either-or. Every element of a brand-marketing program should build demand for your company and its products. In turn, all your demand generation efforts should reinforce and strengthen your company's brand. Unfortunately, there are many misconceptions about the role of brand in a company's marketing mix.

> *Brand building is a luxury—we'll invest in it*
> *once our business improves.*
> *Brand is impossible to measure.*
> *We have enough brand awareness. What we need is sales.*
> *Product success is more important than brand success.*

Sound familiar? Some executives still believe brand means a big, expensive advertising campaign that's difficult to measure and only done sporadically when there's extra money in the budget.

The reality is we need to work to accomplish three things:

1. Grow brand awareness

2. Generate leads and impact the bottom line, and

3. Retain customers and make them your biggest advocates . . . all at the same time[7]

We need to make our marketing programs work harder and smarter, far beyond just driving demand for sales. Rather than have three program dials (*brand, demand, expand*) in competition with one another, we need each to work in harmony with one another. The best marketing programs are those that incorporate a brand promise (BMW: *The Ultimate Driving Machine*), a specific product offer (the luxury BMW M3, zero to 60 mph in 4.0 seconds, from $64,000), and a reason for customers to stay (make it your own with BMW credits and options). A marketing leader with integrated marketing know-how is invaluable in optimizing your marketing programs.

Here are some proven ways to *amp up* the marketing program dial:

1. **Be planful.** Nike's famous slogan "Just Do It" is really bad advice when it comes to running marketing campaigns. All marketing programs should be part of a larger marketing strategy. In turn, all marketing strategies should align with your company's business strategy. (We identified planning as one of the six core marketing processes in Chapter 8.) One-off or ad hoc tactics, regardless of how tempting or clever the idea, usually waste time and money. They often leave customers confused and do little to build a consistent customer experience. Aim to be clear, instead of clever. Aim to be reliable, instead of spontaneous.

2. **Go deep.** You have two choices when dividing your marketing program budget into campaigns: go wide or go

deep. Marketers go wide when they use a *shotgun approach*, launching a large number of small campaigns in the hope that some of them will hit the target. Marketers go deep when they use a *rifle approach*, launching a small number of large campaigns aimed at a narrowly defined target audience and objective. For the resource-challenged organization, the rifle approach is the better choice. Using the earlier $7 million program budget example, it is far better to launch seven campaigns with $1 million heft behind each, than launch seventy campaigns each funded at $100,000. Not only are seven campaigns easier to manage, measure, and tweak, but the larger investment makes for a larger impact and more integrated dialogue with your targeted audience.

3. **Be consistent**. Marketing is like exercise—you'll get better results when you make it part of your routine. Avoid stop-and-start marketing. Going in and out of market in spurts is counterproductive and wasteful. A consistent and persistent presence with your target audience demonstrates that your brand is a reliable choice with staying power. If your company has a blog, make sure you post on a consistent schedule. It doesn't matter if you blog twice a week or once a month; the important thing is consistency. Same is true for customer publications, newsletters, social media marketing, and partner and customer events. Consistency builds great brands.

Turning the Dial on BUDGETS

It's amazing to me how many marketing budgets are *locked up* in long-term commitments. Then, when a challenging quarter or business downturn hits, we have nowhere to cut but our demand-driving-revenue-producing campaigns. Needless to say, that's not the budget tradeoff that management is looking for.

Multiyear sponsorships, agency retainers, long-term contracts, ongoing consulting engagements, co-op advertising allowances, brand tracking studies, legacy marketing infrastructure, internal charge-backs, and other *contractually obligated* line items limit our marketing agility.

Here's an example: McDonald's recently terminated its forty-one-year Olympic sponsorship three years early, as part of a review of its marketing spend and a *new global growth plan.*[8] Imagine having a fixed marketing line item in the budget—estimated at $25 million a year—for more than forty years! Think of all the other marketing opportunities that may have been missed as a result.

Compare McDonald's approach to that of Coca-Cola. Coke focuses 70 percent of its resources (*time, energy, effort, money*) on tried-and-true investments that are working, 20 percent on scaling experimental investments, and 10 percent on new bets. If something works, it is analyzed and scaled up as much and as rapidly as possible. If the return is minimal, it is discarded. And it all has to happen quickly and become part of an ongoing, rapid cycle of experimentation, measurement, and execution.[9]

While there may be a sound rationale and strong ROI for each of our fixed expenses, they tie our hands from seizing a customer insight moment. These *moments of truth*, as they are called, are choice interactions between a customer and a company that leave a lasting positive or negative impression. These are moments in the customer's journey when there is a high level of emotional energy in the outcome. It could be a stranded traveler, lost order, damaged shipment, missing part, erroneous invoice, confusing diagnosis, or faulty product. Engaging and responding in real-time requires an agile organization with some budget flexibility. That's hard to do when all your resources are *locked up* elsewhere.

How do we move the dial from less fixed dollars to more variable dollars that improve our marketing agility? I've used the following four strategies with good success:

1. **Benchmark industry best practices.** All the major consulting firms conduct research on the optimal marketing investment mix. These benchmarks are often broken down by industry (manufacturing, education, technology, etcetera), by type of business (product or service), by primary audience served (B2B or B2C), and a host of other factors. They are often further broken down by elements of the marketing mix (brand building, events, digital marketing, etcetera).

   There are many good analyses that detail what percent of total marketing spend peer companies are investing in brand versus demand, for example, as well as by key marketing categories. Use these benchmarks to educate and influence your marketing teams and encourage more strategic budgeting decisions.

2. **Implement governance and financial controls.** Your top five marketing spend categories typically account for 80 percent of your total marketing spend. Identify and start with these five and put in place a lightweight governance model for each. This should include the *policy*, *process* and *metrics* that will be used across your company.

   For example, you may institute a *policy* that any new sponsorship requires signoff by the CMO, or that all media spend needs to go through a named agency of record. Next, detail the *approval process* that's required and any needed *exception process* to deal with escalations. Then, specify the *metrics* you will use to ensure compliance. An example of such a measure might be the percent of your total spend that flows through approved suppliers or the percentage of your total marketing dollars allocated to events versus digital versus social and the like.

3. **Re-evaluate financial spending authority limits.** The third way to free up fixed costs is to tighten up signing authority and spending limits across the marketing team. Most finance departments have clear guidelines covering

this. Having fewer marketing budget owners overall certainly simplifies things. If that's not practical, you may want to limit any marketing expenditures over a certain dollar amount to individuals at a director or VP level. Or that any multiyear marketing commitment requires review and approval by the CMO.

There are a number of financial controls you can put in place to avoid falling into the fixed budget trap. Finance can be one of your most powerful allies here. The person who holds the funds should never have the authority to make decisions in isolation about how they are used. Imposing spending authority limits is not meant to reduce individual empowerment; rather, it is good management. We should never forget that we are merely stewards of our company's funds; it's not our money.

4. **Implement an approved supplier list**. Another powerful ally for marketing is your procurement team. Procurement organizations support the sourcing activities, negotiation, and strategic selection of goods and services that are important to a company. They often manage the process of selecting vendors, establishing payment terms, negotiating contracts, and ensuring goods and services are delivered as agreed.

   Most marketing organizations suffer from an overabundance of marketing suppliers, many used on a piecemeal or tactical basis. Why is that a bad thing? For starters, it increases the amount of financial transactions that need to be processed, decreases the opportunity for volume discounts and cost savings, and requires more of your time to supervise and to manage.

   Partner with your procurement team to implement an *approved supplier list* (ASL) based on a competitive bid process and with clear agency performance criteria. Depending on the size and complexity of your organization, an ASL can be a formally or informally kept list.

Its purpose is to ensure a roster of best-in-class suppliers available for use across your entire business. An ASL can help eliminate redundant sourcing efforts, negotiate better pricing, and achieve higher standards of quality, service, and delivery. It can also provide an early warning signal to prevent problems with a supplier from repeating across multiple organizations.

Turning the Dial on AGENCIES

The final dial marketers can use to optimize their agility is *agencies*. I make an intentional distinction here between suppliers and agency partners. While all agencies are suppliers, not all suppliers are agencies. We often look to suppliers to execute tools and tactics; we look to agencies to be a strategic partner.

Engaging agencies as strategic partners—rather than as vendors or suppliers—improves brand consistency, quality standards, and purchasing leverage. Rather than engage them in one-off deliverables, *agency partners are most effective when they know how all the deliverables tie together*.

In marketing, the fewer agencies you deploy the better. Not only is it easier to manage a smaller cadre of agencies, but it can dramatically make your marketing more efficient and more effective. Most companies, however, suffer from an unchecked proliferation of suppliers and agencies.

For example, take Unilever again. With 3,000 agencies, and more than 400 brands, the company suffered from agency creep. Unilever recently set out to halve the number of agencies with which it works, investing more with their strategic agencies.[10] Chief marketing and communications officer Keith Weed believes the consumer shouldn't pay more for inefficiency and is aggressively eliminating waste at agencies. "We should get the best price for our consumers. And if that means rooting out inefficiencies in someone else's business, I will do it," he says.

Procter & Gamble is on a similar warpath. In 2009, P&G spent around $1 billion on agency fees and had 2,500 marketing-services agencies. In 2015, the company announced a major agency consolidation with a goal of saving $500 million annually in agency fees and production costs. The goal wasn't just to consolidate, but also to "improve the lineup, so our brands are working with the best talent in the world," says Marc Pritchard, P&G's global brand officer.[11]

P&G's first wave of agency consolidation worked. In its recent fiscal year, the company cut the number of agencies it works with by 40 percent globally and trimmed agency and production spending by around 15 percent, or $300 million. And that was just year one. The marketing savings also helped P&G beat the company's earnings estimates despite soft sales.[12]

In 2018, P&G announced a further round of cuts to its agency roster. The consumer packaged goods company plans to "reinvent" its relationship with agencies and automate and in-house more media planning, buying, and distribution. The move would cut agencies by another 50 percent, saving an additional $400 million.[13]

Agencies are facing a similar challenge, which is giving way to an interesting dynamic. While agencies are often perceived as cost drivers, big professional services and IT consulting firms—the likes of Accenture, Deloitte, IBM, KPMG, McKinsey, and PricewaterhouseCoopers—are positioning themselves as cost savers. These global consultancies are buying up old-guard advertising agencies and reshaping the brand marketing world.[14]

In the past few years, Accenture has grown its operations to include 18,000 digital and creative professionals worldwide. Brian Whipple, head of Accenture Interactive, says, "Brands are now created by a series of connected—or often disconnected—experiences (consumers have) with a company across multiple channels. This requires a new level of connectivity between marketing/creative, business and digital/technology. Clients are coming to us looking for the merger of these three worlds."

The trend toward consolidation, on the client side and on the agency side, is predicted only to accelerate.

Less Is More

How many agencies do you need? Clearly Unilever and P&G found their sprawl of agencies inefficient and took steps to strategically consolidate. We found a similar pattern during a marketing transformation I led across HP. At the time, HP had more than 3,000 marketing suppliers around the globe. Working with my counterparts in procurement and finance, we discovered our top fifteen suppliers made up 49 percent of the company's total marketing spend. The remaining 3,046 suppliers made up 51 percent of spend.

Do you think the top fifteen suppliers or the next 3,046 were easier to manage and provided HP with greater economies of scale, brand cohesion, leverage, and attention? Obviously it is the former and not the latter.

Which leads me back to the original question: How many agencies do you need? Clearly no one agency can do it all (though many claim they can), and *more* has shown to be inefficient and ineffective. I believe most midsize companies are adequately served by engaging no more than six agencies with the following specialties:

1. **Branding/Creative/Media**: to help you focus your brand and develop brilliant creative concepts and placements

2. **Public Relations/Analyst Relations**: to help you quickly build external relationships and begin to establish thought leadership

3. **Digital Marketing/Web Design**: to help you synthesize your story and offerings in an engaging manner online and through social channels

4. **Core Marcom Deliverables**: to help you create the foundational marketing, sales, and employee engagement materials—from collateral to presentations to posters

5. **Event Management**: to help you create and deliver world-class experiences—physical, virtual, or hybrid

6. **Video/Film Production**: to help you develop multisensory, experiential assets that bring your brand to life for both your employees and your customers

In addition to these six specialties, you may also want to engage a few freelance experts to fill a specific need such as a CEO speechwriter or PowerPoint whiz.

Fewer, deeper agency relationships have shown time and time again to be the smarter choice, not just for large multinational companies but for companies of all sizes.

Summary

In a February 2017 CMO survey published by the American Marketing Association, Duke University, and Deloitte pegged marketing spend as a percentage of company revenue at 8.1 percent overall (ranging from 6.9 percent for B2B services companies to 12.4 percent for B2C product companies).[15] That investment typically covers people, programs, budgets, and agencies—the four *Marketing Flexology* dials.

With marketing representing such a large portion of overall company expenditures, marketing budgets will continue to come under intense scrutiny. Don't expect that scrutiny to go away. Instead, focus on becoming the most *nimble, lean, effective, accountable*, and *learning* marketing team possible. How you deploy your marketing resources will determine how seamlessly you can react to unplanned change.

A marketing structure that is light on fixed costs and heavy on variable costs not only allows you to easily pivot based on seasonality or business performance, but it also allows you to capitalize on those rare *moments of truth* in your customer's journey.

Chapter 9 Key Takeaways:

- It doesn't matter how many resources you have. If you don't know how to use them, they will never be enough.

- Nontraditional employment options are often a win-win: They provide employees with greater job flexibility and employers with greater budget control.

- Brand marketing and demand marketing are not an either-or. Both are needed to achieve your company's business goals.

- A flexible marketing budget is a smart marketing budget.

- Agencies are least effective when engaged in one-off deliverables and most effective when they know how all the deliverables tie together.

- Although marketing's relationship with finance and procurement is often tenuous and at odds, it's best to make them your allies.

Chapter 10

MARKETING FLEXOLOGY TOOLS

"We shape our tools and afterwards our tools shape us."
—Marshall McLuhan

In this chapter, we cover the fourth and final step in becoming a marketing agility powerhouse. To recap, in Step 1, we adopted a *business-first mindset* along with five winning traits. In Step 2, we laid a strong and flexible marketing foundation comprised of three core elements: *purpose*, *people*, and *process*. In Step 3, we fine-tuned our four marketing dials: *people*, *programs*, *budgets*, and *agencies*. And now in Step 4, the final step of the *Marketing Flexology* management framework, we will implement five surefire tools to increase our likelihood of delivering superb marketing, the first time and every time.

MINDSET	FOUNDATION	DIALS	TOOLS
Business-First	Purpose	People	Communications Brief
Five Traits	People	Programs	Messaging Framework
	Process	Budgets	Marketing Playbook
		Agencies	Executive Dashboard
			Project Management Office

There are two things marketers have in short supply: time and money. Even then, many marketers seem to find time and money to repeat things. It's called rework. And it often results in missed deadlines, wasted time, increased costs, lost customers, and dejected teams.

Fortunately, most rework is preventable if three things are in place: (1) an agreed-to process and tools, (2) employees who follow the process and use the tools, and (3) managers who enforce the process and tools.

When I talk about tools, I'm not referring to the array of marketing automation tools and technologies that now tip the scale at a whopping 5,381.[1] Rather, I'm talking about those core strategic marketing tools every marketing leader needs in their management arsenal to maximize their team's effectiveness.

We lightly touched on this topic in Chapter 8 when I stated most marketers hate the idea of a process. In fact, we hate anything that pins us down or limits our creative freedom. Of course, deep down we know process is a necessary evil to turn a potential free-for-all into a smooth operation with demonstrable ROI . . . as long as it is lightweight, simple, and makes our lives easier.

To that end, here are five tried-and-true basics that will help you save time, money, aggravation, and rework:

1. Communications Brief

2. Messaging Framework

3. Marketing Playbook

4. Executive Dashboard

5. Project Management Office (PMO)

Let's unpack each one at greater length.

The Communications Brief

When I started my marketing career, the communications brief was akin to the prime directive. No work could be initiated without a thoughtfully crafted and vetted brief. My management took it seriously and, as a result, I took it seriously as well.

It is unprofessional and unacceptable to rely solely on a verbal exchange of information. Yet most marketers do. During my stint working on the agency side, I even had clients send major project requests via voicemail and text message. There are a myriad of reasons (or excuses) for bypassing the important communications brief and briefing step, including:

> *The agency already understands what's needed.*
> *I'm under the gun to get this out the door.*
> *This project is on a fast-track.*
> *Let the agency write the brief—that's what I'm paying them for.*
> *I don't want to limit my agency's creativity.*

That's not how to get the best work out of your agency partners or your own internal staff. The adage rings true: Clients get the work they deserve.

Communications Brief: What It Is

A communications brief is an agreement document that guides communication across all key contact points, internal and external. It provides a vital link between business objectives and creative strategies. It ensures a common understanding for any communications project and the investment of time and money that accompanies it, prior to the start of the project.

Communications Brief: Why It's Important

The communications brief:

- Builds alignment internally on important communication challenges and goals

- Helps clarify our thinking and makes us more strategic

- Allows those developing the communication piece to perform better and apply their creativity within the laid-out guidelines

- Minimizes the subjective *I like, I don't like* conversation when evaluating a creative piece

- Eliminates confusion, misunderstandings, multiple revisions, and lackluster results

Communications Brief: What It Contains

Dozens of briefing templates are available to download from the Internet, or you can design your own. Regardless of whether your communications brief is for a product, business, brand, or event, it should cover the following seven areas:

1. **Background:** Describe the current situation and the goals for this project.

2. **Objective:** Include the business and communications objective.

3. **Target Audience:** Identify the user or target audience, including their current perception of your product, brand, or company.

4. **Promise and Proof:** Delineate what sets your product, brand, or company apart and why your target audience should believe you.

5. **Key Message:** Distill your key selling point or differentiator into a single most persuasive idea and call to action.

6. **Timing and Other Parameters:** Specify the timeline and any budget limitations for this piece, how you will evaluate success, and who will provide final approval.

7. **Guidelines:** List any creative guidelines (such as tone and manner) or restrictions that need to be followed.

Agencies are problem solvers, not inventors. They work best when they have a clear problem that needs to be solved. A well-crafted and concise communications brief can save you hours and hours of frustration, rework, and added costs.

The Messaging Framework

Whether you're trying to grow a brand, turn around a company, or deliver a seamless experience, getting everybody moving in the same direction can be challenging. With differing goals, agendas, bosses, and budgets, messages can quickly become fragmented.

How do you prevent message fragmentation? It's certainly not by taking away budgets or by funneling everything through a central headquarters for approval. Message integration doesn't require centralization or budget consolidation. However, it does require leadership, persistence, and a messaging framework.

A messaging framework can help you turn a cacophony of voices into a beautifully synchronized performance. The messaging framework defines why you exist, why people come to you, and what ultimately makes people want to buy your product. Everything you create, internally and externally, should lead back to this messaging.

Messaging Framework: What It Is

A *messaging framework*—sometimes called a *messaging architecture* or *message map*—is a set of statements arranged hierarchically to convey an organization's messaging priorities. It embodies the core positioning of your company and its offerings. With a strong messaging framework, any employee should be able to talk intelligently and confidently about her organization's products, services, and company. It doesn't matter if they are answering the phone, greeting a guest, delivering a presentation, briefing an analyst, or closing a deal.

Messaging Framework: Why It's Important

A messaging framework:

- Helps focus and amplify our core messages
- Aligns our organization around our company's narrative
- Guides our messaging across every piece of content and every channel
- Reduces ad hoc and one-off messages that can confuse our various audiences
- Results in more cohesive, synchronized, and impactful communications

Messaging Framework: What It Contains

The #1 rule when crafting a messaging framework is that it is not about you. You need to move beyond simple feature/function/benefit statements to messaging that demonstrates how you solve a real customer problem better than anyone else. That starts with knowing your target audience and their fears, frustrations, pain points, and deepest needs.

A messaging framework should answer who you are, what you provide both tangible and intangible, for whom, why anyone should care, and what sets you apart. It is typically crafted in hierarchical order, starting with a positioning statement and ending with a concise elevator pitch.

As with the communication brief, you can leverage numerous messaging frameworks. Some are very basic, while others are quite elaborate and complex. I prefer a one-page-at-a-glance format covering the following:

1. **Positioning Statement:** State your mission and brand promise at a high level.

2. **Target Audience:** Identify who you are trying to appeal to and what they are like.

3. **Tone of Voice:** Describe how the character of your business comes through in your written *and* spoken words— is it friendly and straightforward or sophisticated and professional?

4. **What You Do:** Articulate the value you provide when someone buys your product or service.

5. **Why It Matters:** State the customer problem you must solve or need you must address.

6. **How You Do It Better:** List three key attributes that differentiate you from other companies or offerings in the market: Are you the highest quality, best value, most dependable?

7. **Supporting Messages:** Provide three proof points or examples for each of the three attributes you identified in #6 (nine data-rich statements total).

8. **Elevator Pitch:** Include a three-second message that serves as an attention grabber along with a thirty-second message.

Once your messaging framework is completed and approved, post and distribute it broadly throughout your organization, not just to the marketing ranks. Anyone and everyone can be a potential messenger for your company. There's a better chance of getting your message right with a strategic messaging framework.

Marketing Playbook

In sports, a playbook outlines a team's strategies, tactics, and plays. It is an invaluable tool in propelling a team toward victory. Sports teams win championships with the flawless execution of great playbooks. A playbook is not only an indispensable tool for sports teams, but also for winning in the game of business.

In business, as in sports, it pays to be prepared. While customer service and sales commonly rely on playbooks, they are not as prevalent in marketing. Having predetermined responses helps customer service and sales representatives respond consistently and quickly to frequently asked customer questions, objections, and concerns. Customer service playbooks, also known as scripts, predefine the service experience through a series of *if/ then* statements. For example, *if* the customer is unhappy with their purchase for whatever reason, *then* offer a full refund, no questions asked. Sales playbooks provide a common framework and process for closing sales more effectively. Research, in fact, shows that companies with a defined formal sales process grow revenue 18 percent faster than those who don't.[2]

Why would marketing leaders choose to run blindly?

Marketing Playbook: What It Is

A marketing playbook is a detailed reference document that is widely distributed across the marketing community and its key stakeholders, typically on an annual basis with quarterly refreshes throughout the year. It is a living document that helps unify and direct a diverse or global team toward a common goal with a set of useable near-term strategies. While not a substitute for training, a marketing playbook can significantly speed up the onboarding process for new marketing professionals.

In essence, a marketing playbook serves as a global positioning system (GPS) for your team. It helps them navigate unfamiliar or tough terrain 24/7, anywhere in the world.

Marketing Playbook: Why It's Important

The marketing playbook:

- Demonstrates that leadership understands what it takes for a marketing professional to be successful

- Drives focus, consistency, and integration

- Helps team members make smart, coordinated choices under pressure

- Allows for more efficient campaign execution, especially at the local level

- Speeds up the onboarding process for new marketing professionals

Marketing Playbook: What It Contains

General George S. Patton said, "Never tell people how to do things. Tell them what to do and they will surprise you with their ingenuity." Same is true for the marketing playbook. It should guide your team on the overall goals and what's expected, but not instruct them on how to do their jobs.

A marketing playbook should give your team the guidance, tools, and resources to produce nothing short of brilliant marketing. Your playbook should include the following ten chapters:

1. **Introduction:** basic information your marketing professionals need to know, including your company's strategy, mission, vision, and core values

2. **Audience Personas:** a prioritized list of your target audiences along with detailed personas of their needs, wants, and habits

3. **Marketing Game Plan:** the key marketing priorities and initiatives for the year

4. **Key Messages:** here's where your messaging framework (tool #2) comes in

5. **Outcomes:** the expected metrics that will determine success or failure, as well as how common metrics should be calculated and reported

6. **Governance:** any needed review, approval, and checkpoints required

7. **Lightweight Processes/Tools:** many companies today employ some sort of marketing automation software or tool—for scheduling emails to automating social media posts to tracking the lifecycle of customers in their marketing funnel; cover the instructions in this chapter of the Marketing Playbook

8. **Available Assets:** the brand, visual and content assets available for leverage, typically housed in a content management system (CMS) or digital asset management (DAM) system

9. **Campaign Calendar and Checklist:** a link to the master marketing planning calendar that highlights key launch and campaign windows

10. **Available Resources:** who to contact for more information or consultation; typically a list of those individuals who have contributed to the development of the marketing playbook

While developing a marketing playbook requires an extra dose of coordination, collaboration, and effort, the results in terms of consistency, focus, enhanced customer experience, and improved marketing effectiveness are too compelling to ignore. It's what marketing champions do to win their unfair share—mindshare, market share, and share of customer wallet. In the words of Spanish novelist Miguel de Cervantes, "To be prepared is half the victory."

The Executive Dashboard

All metrics are not created equal. Your web team needs to know the load time of your company's website, while your social media team needs to track the number of likes, shares, and comments from your most recent social media post. But does your CEO? Probably not. Communicating the right metrics to the right audience is a critical role of marketing leadership.

Time-constrained executives won't wade through mountains of data or suffer through presentations on marketing performance. An executive dashboard helps you communicate the most critical key performance indicators (KPIs) your execs care about in a concise, actionable, and visually appealing manner.

Executive Dashboard: What It Is

An executive dashboard is different than a marketing score-card. While the two terms are often used interchangeably, they serve different purposes and audiences. Used together, they are a hard-hitting combination for communicating and measuring marketing expectations and performance.

Similar to the dashboard in your car, an *executive dashboard* highlights the important things your executive team needs to be informed about—gas, oil, battery, speed, distance, and temperature. A *marketing scorecard*, on the other hand, displays performance information at a glance, similar to the scoreboard that keeps tally at sporting events—current score, inning, fouls, yards to go, and time remaining on the clock.

While the dashboard and the scorecard focus on performance information, the executive dashboard additionally focuses on the performance expectations of your CEO. That's why it's such an important management tool.

Executive Dashboard: Why It's Important

The executive dashboard:

- Reinforces the link between business objectives and marketing objectives

- Provides an at-a-glance snapshot of marketing's performance to senior management

- Monitors the impact marketing is having on reputation, revenue, sales pipeline, and customer retention

- Allows management to ask the right questions and identify impacts

- Improves communication, confidence, and transparency between the executive ranks and marketing

Executive Dashboard: What It Contains

An executive dashboard is not a report on progress or status of current projects or upcoming events. Rather, it is a snapshot that addresses questions the C-suite is most concerned about, namely what's working, what isn't, and is our marketing investment paying off. Keep these five tips in mind when developing your executive dashboard:

1. **Language:** You develop an executive dashboard for your executives. That means it needs to focus on business outcomes and include metrics that use the standard language of business . . . accounting. The Wharton School of the University of Pennsylvania asserts "The story of any company, no matter the size, the industry, or the country of origin, is told through its financial records and reports. Income, debt, revenue versus expenses, compensation, and cost of retaining customers can all be found on financial statements."[3] Financial data is understood by any individual in the business world—from investors to employees. Using existing financial data as the basis for

your marketing metrics will ensure it is widely understood across the organization and respected for its accuracy.

2. **Strategy:** Here's your opportunity to demonstrate your strategic sense. Good marketing dashboards show a direct link between business goals and marketing outcomes. They tie into KPIs that your executive team tracks on an ongoing basis. Executive dashboards should provide only information that's useful, not what's readily available. Through data, words, and visuals, dashboards can tell a story of how well marketing is advancing the business and financial objectives of your organization.

3. **Metrics:** The metrics your executive dashboard includes will depend on the role marketing plays within your respective organization. Is your role that of a *marketing service provider*, serving as an in-house marketing agency for the company? Does your team function as a *marketing advisor* to the CEO and executive team, primarily on brand and reputation matters? Or is marketing's role to be a business partner and *driver of new growth?* (I cover each of these roles in detail in Chapter 8). Executive dashboard metrics can range from building reputation and brand to generating qualified leads, to attracting and retaining customers, to driving product adoption, and to enhancing the customer experience. An executive dashboard is another great opportunity to have a dialogue with your C-suite and gain alignment on marketing's greatest value add.

4. **Objective:** Use objective measures, rather than subjective measures, in your dashboard. Subjective measures are focused on outputs—counting how many things we've produced, be it events, collateral pieces, or campaigns. Subjective measures focus on efficiency—did we deliver on time, on budget? While these are good variables to keep on the radar, they are not the measures that matter most to your executive team. Objective measures are stronger, focusing on outcomes (rather than outputs), return on investment (rather than completion), customer advocacy

(rather than internal client satisfaction), and effectiveness (rather than efficiency).

5. **Visualization:** The format of your executive dashboard can be as important as the information it contains. The best dashboards are communicated on one page or one screen. Ensure your dashboard flows in a logical manner from left to right, from top to bottom. Dashboards that are visually appealing and uncluttered are also more inviting and can be easier to digest. Go easy on the footnotes and disclaimers—they will make your results appear shaky or unconfirmed. Engaging a graphic designer to produce your final executive dashboard is time and money well spent. Studies have shown that the human brain processes images 60,000 times faster than text, and 90 percent of information transmitted to the brain is visual.[4] Use this to good advantage in visualizing your executive dashboard.

Despite their merits, executive dashboards do have their drawbacks. While they convey snapshots of important measures, they are poor at providing the nuance and context that effective data-driven decision making demands. They can even lead managers to incorrect conclusions.[5] For instance, one number on its own—such as the number of sales leads—without additional context doesn't really tell your executives whether they should laugh or cry. This is where comparative or trending data is useful. Dashboards also do a poor job of predicting future events based on past data or prescribing a course of action. Because of this, executive dashboards work best when used as a *discussion starter,* coupled with one-on-one meetings with your executive team.

The Project Management Office

The final tool in the *Marketing Flexology* arsenal is the PMO. When I think about a PMO, I usually think of it as something deployed in large, global decentralized companies. PMOs are absolutely a staple of big companies in driving enterprise-scale change initiatives. But they can also benefit small and midsize organizations. There are many different PMO models, but they generally fall into one of two camps: (1) a standing PMO or (2) an ad hoc PMO.

A standing PMO typically reports into a VP of strategy and is focused on bridging the gap between a company's strategic vision and implementation of that vision. The standing PMO often focuses on process and operational improvements and is accountable for the resulting cost savings produced. The percentage of organizations with an active or standing PMO is trending up—from 61 percent in 2007 to 71 percent in 2017.[6] Yet, more than half of all CEOs are not prepared to adopt the new changes that a standing PMO wants to implement.[7]

On the other hand, an ad hoc PMO comes together to tackle a specific challenge or defined problem, often assigned by the CEO. It could be a digital transformation, a new growth initiative, a process simplification, a companywide budget reduction, a reorganization, or any large-scale change initiative. With an ad hoc PMO, a cross-functional team is assembled then disbanded after the initiative is complete. Peter Bendor-Samuel, CEO of the Everest Group, describes the difference between the two as an "authoritative PMO" versus a "coaching PMO."

Project Management Office: What It Is

There are almost as many models of PMOs as there are companies implementing them. I've been involved with a number of PMOs over my career. I played a lead role in three of them: One focused on building the marketing workforce of the future (roles, skills, experience, centers of excellence), the second in transforming a distributed 5,000-person marketing contingent into an integrated powerhouse, and the third in delivering $172 million in marketing savings through smart consolidation. Additionally, I've led several companywide brand repositionings.

In each instance, the mission was clear: (1) assemble a group of high-performing individuals across multiple businesses and functions, (2) solve a specific problem or drive a companywide initiative, (3) use an efficient and effective process, and (4) produce exceptional results.

Project Management Office: Why It's Important

A project management office:

- Defines a common language, provides structure, and brings standardization across the company

- Delivers economies of scale by creating consistent systems and processes

- Provides an objective and transparent source of truth from which to base decisions

- Solves an important companywide problem or challenge

- Identifies best practices that can be leveraged across the company

Project Management Office: What It Contains

Creating and leading a successful PMO requires the following key elements:

1. **Right participants:** Ensure your PMO is staffed with empowered participants. Send a note to the senior-most person in each business unit and function outlining the goals of the PMO and requesting that an empowered individual be assigned to represent their interests. If you have a specific recommendation, state who you would ideally like to have included.

2. **Executive sponsorship and engagement:** The best PMOs are driven by a burning initiative that is on the CEO's radar. That doesn't mean your CEO needs to be actively

involved, but it does mean he or she needs to be visible at key milestones. It can take the form of ten minutes to set the stage at the initial kick-off meeting, an unannounced drop-in during a PMO meeting, participating in key report outs, or even a REPLY ALL to a meeting recap with encouragement, praise, or additional direction.

3. **Clarity:** A successful marketing PMO has clear goals, time horizons, deliverables, and outcomes. Are participants signing up for three weeks or three years? Is this a full-time commitment or a nights-and-weekends commitment? Spell it out to eliminate any misunderstandings. This applies to participants as well as to the executive team. Make sure everyone is on the same page.

4. **Ground rules:** At the start of a PMO, set some ground rules. One ground rule I always insisted on is having empowered decision makers in the room; another is that the meetings start and stop on time. You might choose a *no delegate* policy. It is sometimes useful to set these ground rules together as a team, at the inaugural PMO meeting.

5. **Stellar project management:** Nothing makes or breaks a PMO faster than project management or lack thereof. This includes (1) a dedicated scribe, which allows the PMO leader to fully engage in the meetings, (2) a tight agenda with report outs, status updates, milestones achieved, and next steps from each participant, (3) timely meeting notes that capture and track actions, decisions made, decisions needed, and dependencies, and (4) periodic executive-level communications sent to all business units and functional leaders, letting them know of the PMO's progress and thanking them for their ongoing support.

A survey conducted by PricewaterhouseCoopers found that a third of all PMOs failed to meet their desired results. Reasons included inadequate project estimating and planning (30 percent of the project failures), a lack of executive sponsorship (16 percent of the failures), and poorly defined goals and objectives (12 percent). By following the five criteria just discussed, your PMO will have a better chance of delivering real business benefit to your organization and your C-suite.

Adopting these five time-tested tools will add rigor and structure to your marketing organization. Your team will appreciate established processes and tools at their disposal to get their work done. The trick is to keep the tools lightweight, flexible, and simple to encourage adoption. There are a few additional tools I would recommend implementing once you have these vital five up and running. They include an *editorial calendar*, a *content map*, *marketing lexicon*, *customer journey map*, and *agency briefing checklist*. I provide how-to insight on these—and other—tools on my website: www.marketingflexology.com. Check back often for the latest insight and tools.

In the next chapter, we put the four-step *Marketing Flexology* management framework into practice, with a week-by-week action plan and a ninety-day challenge.

Summary

I'm quick to adopt new systems, processes, and tools that free up time, energy, and mental space, whether it improves my commute, reduces food preparation time, organizes my finances, or automates other aspects of my life. But I don't believe you can cut corners, in life or in marketing. Finding shortcuts is resourceful, but not if it eliminates key steps or compromises the final outcome.

These five core marketing fundamentals are a *must-have* in every good marketing leader's toolkit. These tools will save you time, energy, money, resources, and stress. And you'll have a better chance of producing brilliant marketing for your company and your customers.

Chapter 10 Key Takeaways:

- Stellar marketing requires thoughtful planning. A well-crafted and concise communications brief will save you hours of frustration, rework, and added costs.

- Product features aren't benefits. Ensure your messaging framework demonstrates how you can solve a customer problem better than anyone else.

- A messaging framework is where your company's story begins. As such, creating the right messaging for your company deserves time, thought, and energy.

- An executive dashboard is a simple one-page understanding between you and your executive team of marketing's value and contribution.

- PMOs may be *project management offices* but the "P" in PMO is as much about managing people as it is about managing projects. Learn to balance the two, and you will be wildly successful.

Chapter 11

PUTTING INTO PRACTICE

"The secret to getting ahead is getting started."
—Mark Twain

For too long we've been lulled into believing that marketing is a combination of art and science. In the chapters you've just navigated, I described the modern-day challenges gripping today's business and marketing professionals. Because of these, it is important to shift and update our marketing paradigm for the following reasons:

- Endless streams of customer data with no time to make sense of it all

- A technology landscape tipping the scales at over 5,000 tools

- Digital channels overflowing with content

- Human attention span trailing that of a goldfish

- Ever-faster news cycles

- Open rates in the single digits

- More new marketing hacks than there are marketers

- Performance metrics that are inconsistent between channels

- A practice that now includes bots, AI, and machine learning

- Careers that are measured in months, not years

To address each of these challenges, today's marketing, as I mentioned at the start of this book, requires a mix of insight and agility—well shaken—and served with a splash of creativity. In other words, it requires the new elixir: *Marketing Flexology*. In the previous chapters, I shared detailed steps of this proven and proprietary management framework with you.

The steps include a mental model and an operating model. The *mental model* requires adjusting your mindset, beginning with a commitment to becoming a business-first leader. The challenges just outlined should help you do that. The *operating model* includes three core elements, four dials, and five tools that form the foundation of the *Marketing Flexology* practice. Implementing each one of these will help you move closer to the ultimate goal of *Marketing Flexology*. Furthermore, putting this framework into practice will help you deal with the daily challenges and curveballs that come with being a marketing leader—but only if you take those important first few steps.

My Ninety-Day Challenge

Honestly, I don't want to see you go after coming this far. And I know that once you put this book down you'll be right back at it—fighting the day-to-day battles and ever-increasing demands on you and your team. To use an analogy, it's tough to refuel a plane that's in flight. Together, we can carve out the time and effort to implement these principles into your everyday life and marketing practices.

To help you do that, I'm providing you with a *get started* checklist along with a ninety-day challenge. Why ninety days, you ask? The first ninety days in any new endeavor are referred to as the *make or break, sink or swim,* or *do or die* period. Hiring managers often probe prospective employees to determine what they'll accomplish in their first ninety days on the job, if selected. When beginning a new position, your boss will likely ask you for a thirty/sixty/ninety-day job plan. In the first ninety days, your manager decides whether they made the right hiring decision. Not surprisingly, the ninety-day period also corresponds with the timeframe of when a company reports their financial results for the quarter.

It can take anywhere from two months up to eight months to build a new behavior into your life. And, on average, it takes sixty-six days before a new habit becomes automatic.[1] As with all change, it is a process and not an event. Results can vary widely depending on the behavior change, the person, and the circumstances involved. That's why I am referring to it as a ninety-day *challenge*. But I am confident that the framework outlined in this book will help you move the needle and reach your goals.

Thirty/Sixty/Ninety-Day Action Plan

People with written goals are 50 percent more likely to achieve them than those without. Yet, only three out of every 100 adults write their goals down on paper.[2] Writing it down is key. Those goals held in the mind are more likely to be jumbled up with the 1,500 thoughts per minute the average person experiences. So step one, you must have a written action plan.

I've created a skeleton of an action plan to help you get started on your journey through *Marketing Flexology*. It is a thirty/sixty/ninety-day plan you can customize to meet your unique business, situation, or challenge. Follow this week-by-week guide, and you'll nail your transition to a *Marketing Flexology* mindset and toolset.

The first thirty days are focused on alignment. The next thirty days are when you stand up your new operating model. The final thirty days are when the transformation takes hold.

Your Week-by-Week Guide

Week 1: Schedule a *kick-off* meeting with your extended team (directs plus key internal and external stakeholders).
Goal: Paint a vision, address concerns, secure commitment, present action plan.

Week 2: Conduct a *gap analysis* between current state and future state.
Goal: Identify and prioritize needed areas of focus; assign owners for each.

Week 3: Assess current and potential sources of *customer insights*.
Goal: Become an insight machine; move from lagging indicators to leading indicators; connect with frontline employees; beef up social media listening, online brand communities, and more.

Week 4: Begin incorporating *creativity* and *learning agility* into your team cadence.
Goal: Sharpen your team's focus on creativity and continuous improvement; foster ways to make it habit forming (part of team meetings, performance discussions, metrics, training opportunities).

Week 5: Re-examine (or create) your team's *guiding principles*.
Goal: Establish a common understanding of—and adherence to—your team charter, talent strategies, and core processes.

Week 6: Evaluate and adjust current *marketing head count* across your entire company.
Goal: Aim for a more flexible workforce; adjust the mix of full-time and flexible workers; assess current staffing and future requirements.

Week 7: Evaluate and adjust current *marketing programs* across your entire company.
Goal: Align with business goals; ensure marketing programs are driving demand *and* brand; cut underperforming, non-strategic programs.

Week 8: Evaluate and adjust current *marketing budgets* across your entire company.
Goal: Identify and eliminate unproductive fixed costs, maximize variable costs; calculate and monitor program-to-people ratio; establish any needed policies and financial controls; become best friends with finance.

Week 9: Evaluate and adjust current deployment of *marketing agencies* across your entire company.
Goal: Evaluate and adjust current marketing agencies; initiate any required agency consolidation based on past performance and future need; become best friends with procurement.

Week 10: Create a new (or improved) *executive dashboard.*
Goal: Improve communication, accountability, and transparency between the executive ranks and marketing; couple with one-on-one meetings with your executive team to strengthen marketing-to-business alignment.

Week 11: Develop a *marketing playbook* and other missing *core tools.*
Goal: Align your company's customer-facing employees; enhance the customer experience while improving marketing effectiveness.

Week 12: Review your ninety-day *transformation results* with your extended team and C-suite.
Goal: Review and assess your results with your extended team and members of your C-suite; solicit input and support to sustain your new *Marketing Flexology* practice.

Bravo! You have just kicked your marketing, your team, and your professional career into high gear. Best of all, you've initiated the change instead of waiting for the next marketing shakeup. Remember the CEB-Gartner statistic from Chapter 5? Employees who initiate change have 43 percent more positive impact on their companies than those who just have the capacity to change. You've demonstrated that you are a leader who is *large and in charge.*

At the same time, you've built a marketing foundation that is *nimble* (dexterous in movement and thought), *lean* (no superfluous fat), *effective* (gets the right things done), *accountable* (responsive and responsible), and *learning* (committed to continuous improvement). That foundation will help you surf the tsunami of disruption, change, and accompanying chaos we all will face in the years and decades ahead. Change is inevitable, but preparation is a choice.

Complacency has no place in the new marketing world, nor does mediocrity. It's no longer about *good-fast-cheap, pick two*, but rather about *better-faster-cheaper-smarter, deliver all*. It's not about lying low during a transformation while hoping you and your team emerge unscathed, but rather choosing to be in the eye of the storm driving the needed redesign. The status quo is the archenemy of marketing agility.

Additional Support

Consider this just the beginning of your journey to the new art and science I call *Marketing Flexology*. In your hands you have the know-how and the tools to not only survive, but to thrive in this new future. For sure there will be new responsibilities, new technologies, new channels, and new challenges. Will the road ahead continue to be rocky and uncertain? Most likely. Will it be exhilarating. Absolutely!

I'll be with you on that journey and just one click away. My website, www.marketingflexology.com, serves as a learning hub for marketing agility. Through my articles, free downloads, additional tools, and resources, I hope to advance our collective *Marketing Flexology* know-how and expertise.

Let's stay connected, shall we?

Recap of Key Takeaways

Here are the takeaways from each of the preceding chapters. Consider these your *Marketing Flexology* CliffsNotes.[3]

- **Chapter 1:** The marketing *art and science* of yesteryear has been superseded by today's demand for a 24/7 customer lifeline that we can turn into action faster than competitors. *Insight and agility* are the new art and science.

- **Chapter 2:** Successful marketers create their own calls to action. Don't wait for a crisis to initiate change.

- **Chapter 3:** The best way to gain understanding and meaningful insight into your customer is to go directly to the source. Up-close-and-personal trumps trailing insight any day.

- **Chapter 4:** Changing directions without missing a beat, breaking a sweat, or losing your job—that's what marketing agility is all about.

- **Chapter 5:** How we respond to unexpected upheaval can determine our success or failure. The best way to avert change is to initiate it. Will you shakeup the status quo, or will you wait to be shaken?

- **Chapter 6:** In a profession that is becoming increasingly automated, robotic, and self-driving, I'd place my bet on creativity. Creativity is marketing's best career insurance.

- **Chapter 7:** I can teach you the skills and give you the tools, but without the right mindset you will never achieve your optimal marketing potential.

- **Chapter 8:** Marketing principles serve as guardrails for our organizations. With a strong foundation, marketers can weather most business fluctuations.

- **Chapter 9:** While there are many variables outside of marketing's control, these four dials are all ours—*people, programs, budgets*, and *agencies*.

- **Chapter 10:** Get it right the first time by adopting these five tried-and-true marketing tools guaranteed to save you time, money, frustration and needless rework: communications brief, messaging framework, marketing playbook, executive dashboard, and project management office.

- **Chapter 11:** Getting started is the first step. With my week-by-week guide and ninety-day challenge, you have nothing to lose and everything to gain. What are you waiting for?

Use these key takeaways as lighthouses to guide you to land as you navigate the torrential waters in front of you. Each one has its place and offers tremendous value to your development, success, and *Marketing Flexology*.

CONCLUSION

"My mission in life is not merely to survive, but to thrive."
—Maya Angelou

In the beginning of this book, I shared that a powerful drive to survive shaped my outlook and marketing methods. Over many years of marketing practice, I frequently had to justify my results, defend my budget, submit contingency plans, explain the value of my organization, and shield my team and agency partners. During tough times, my survival instinct intensified as company leaders scrounged for areas to cut to meet their promised financial targets. Not surprisingly, a company's marketing and advertising budgets are frequently the first cost cuts. Likewise, CMOs are first in the firing line when growth targets are not met.[1] The words *survival of the fittest* have a special meaning for marketers. We know that only the strongest producing programs and people will continue to be successful and exist while the others will fail and fade away.

After experiencing firsthand hundreds of marketing leaders and how they managed their teams, their budgets, their programs, and their agencies, I came to realize that much of the reinvention chaos and anguish was self-inflicted. Time and again I witnessed leaders who tolerated underperforming team members, endured antiquated processes, maintained runaway budgets, invested in ineffective campaigns, and partnered with suboptimal agencies. Then, during challenging times, their organizations became exposed, warts and all. In these chapters, I've given you a road-map to avoid repeating these same mistakes.

143

It's easy to get caught up in the survival game, especially when there's a lot to keep up with and careers are at stake. We're so busy dodging the bullets, ducking the reinventions, and defending our turf that we have little remaining time to blaze new trails. We know we should propel our careers, our teams, and our marketing to a new, higher level, but we struggle to just keep afloat. How, then, do we make the leap from surviving to thriving? Certainly, putting a *Marketing Flexology* foundation in place will position you to be among the fittest of the marketing fit. And, when business needs demand, *Marketing Flexology* will enable you to quickly and easily change directions . . . without missing a beat, breaking a sweat, or losing your job. That added flexibility should help you carve out some needed space to elevate your marketing for even greater success.

From Survive to Thrive

There's a marked difference between surviving and thriving. Survival is an instinct and reaction to change; thriving is a choice and set of proactive actions to stay ahead of the curve. There is no shortcut or detour to move us from survive to thrive. Rather, it is the number of small actions we take that propel us forward on the road to thriving. In their book *Do One Thing Every Day That Scares You,* authors Robie Rogge and Dian Smith provide a year's worth of fear-facing prompts to challenge our comfort zone. The authors believe that by performing one small act of daring every day—whether it's pitching an idea, asking for help, admitting a mistake, accepting a compliment, going for the prize, failing spectacularly, and trying again, or hundreds of other brave acts—we will cultivate a habit of thinking courageously.

In closing, I'd like to leave you with some small actions that have guided my own marketing journey throughout the years. These are intended to help you make the leap from merely surviving to thriving. Whenever the day-to-day pressures bogged me down, I sought to lift my head—if only for a moment—and take a look back and a look ahead. Doing so helped me gain a needed perspective of where my current challenge fit within the larger marketing continuum.

Learn from the Past

I would have loved practicing marketing during what we nostalgically call the "Mad Men" era of the 1960s. Yes, it is known for its antics and high-voltage culture, but it is also revered as a time of brilliant storytelling. During this era, marketers created some of the most iconic campaigns. Baby boomers were coming of age, disposable income and leisure time were at their highest, and Americans were united in a spirit of hope and optimism.

Who can forget the Avis "we try harder" or Clairol "does she or doesn't she" ads? Who doesn't smile hearing Coca-Cola's multiethnic, peace-promoting "I'd like to teach the world to sing" 1970s' message? Not only did these marketing campaigns break the rules of creativity, they tapped into a deep consumer insight. That's something today's algorithms and A/B testing can't replicate.

I feel privileged to have practiced marketing during some of the most pivotal years in the evolution of our young profession. I cut my marketing teeth during an era of big brands, mass marketing, and mass media. I was subjected to (and threatened with being left behind by) the advent of e-marketing. I saw elevator pitches replaced by hashtags and logos serving double-duty as avatars. I worked alongside *mad men* who became *math men*—practitioners who traded in their creative chops to hone their data and analytic sensibilities. I hope as you reach for that next shiny object, you will also reach back to learn what your marketing ancestors have contributed to the marketing profession.

Throughout these chapters, I cited several marketing pioneers. And I also shared stories from some of the world's leading CEOs and CMOs. These legendary *marketing greats* have changed the face of marketing and deserve our attention. Each of these visionaries broke with the status quo by tapping into a deep consumer insight. If you don't yet know these marketing pioneers, get to know them. You will be inspired by their stories, their contributions, and their lasting legacy to the marketing profession.

Prepare for the Future

No one would call marketing a staid profession. Ever-changing consumer needs, wants, motivations, and behaviors demand ever-changing marketing strategies and tactics. Indeed, this is the allure that draws many of us into the marketing profession. It seems every day we wake up to a new surprise or a new crisis that demands our time and energy. While exhilarating, marketing can easily turn into an endless game of whack-a-mole.

The marketing future has many surprises awaiting us. As time and attention continue to dwindle, consumers will become even more sophisticated and demanding. As technology advancements accelerate, marketers will be forced to continuously re-evaluate how we deliver messages to the market. As business pressures mount, marketing programs and leaders will continue to come under increasing scrutiny. Reality will continue to surprise us, so we need to be ready. The best way I have found to prepare for the future is to have an active hand in shaping it. There are three things you can do today that your future self will thank you for:

Tip # 1: Hone your skills. Experts predict by the year 2034, 47 percent of today's jobs will be automated. Sixty-five percent of today's students will be applying for jobs that don't exist yet.[2] The marketing prowess that landed you your current role will likely be outdated when you are vying for your next one. Commit to being a lifelong learner.

Tip # 2: Become more strategic. After a while, even whack-a-mole becomes tiresome. That's because they keep reappearing no matter how perfectly or heroically you swat them. There's always another marketing challenge demanding of your attention. Working faster or harder is obviously not the answer; we need to become more strategic marketers. Take the time to question how that next urgent marketing request advances a broader marketing strategy and, in turn, how both will help achieve your company's overall business strategy.

Tip # 3: Invest in yourself. Investing time and money in yourself is one of the best return on investments you can make. Not only will it better prepare you for an uncertain future, but there is often a current payoff in terms of career readiness. Whether it's becoming more strategic, more creative, or more agile, take lessons that continue to push you forward and move you out of your comfort zone.

These are the lessons learned to help you move from merely surviving to thriving as a marketing leader: Learn from the past. Prepare for the future. And, above all, continue creating brilliant marketing filled with insight and agility . . . and serve it with a splash.

NOTES (BIBLIOGRAPHY)

Chapter 1

1. "Gartner Survey Reveals Marketing Budgets Increased for Third Consecutive Year," http://www.gartner.com/newsroom/id/3506917

2. "The Rise of the Chief Marketing Technologist," https://hbr.org/2014/07/the-rise-of-the-chief-marketing-technologist

3. "Marketers Must Assume Control of Customer Experience," https://www.marketingweek.com/2014/04/01/marketers-must-assume-control-of-customer-experience/

4. "CMOs Much More Likely Than CIOs to Lead Digital Transformation," http://www.cio.com/article/3121990/cio-role/cmos-much-more-likely-than-cios-to-lead-digital-transform.html

5. "Hyatt Nixes Global CMO Role in Corporate Reshuffling," https://www.marketingdive.com/news/hyatt-nixes-global-cmo-role-in-corporate-reshuffling/515206/

6. "Personality Traits of an Exceptionally Strong CMO," https://www.forbes.com/sites/danielnewman/2016/12/27/personality-traits-of-an-exceptionally-strong-cmo/#212e79793c34

7. "E. Jerome McCarthy," https://en.wikipedia.org/wiki/E._Jerome_McCarthy

8. "AOL's Digital Prophet Claims the Four Ps of Marketing Are Absolute Rubbish," https://www.marketingweek.com/2017/06/16/aol-digital-prophet-david-shing-criticises-outdated-marketers/

9. "New York City Is Using Your Yelp Reviews to Find Health Code Violations," https://www.fastcompany.com/3031043/

fast-feed/new-york-city-is-using-your-yelp-reviews-to-find-health-code-violations

10. "Study: Millennials Are the Most Brand-Loyal Generation," https://www.inc.com/geoff-smith/millennials-becoming-more-loyal-in-era-of-consumer-choice.html

11. "A Brand Manager's Guide to Losing Control," http://hbswk.hbs.edu/item/a-brand-managers-guide-to-losing-control

Chapter 2

1. "Top 10 Companies That Radically Transformed Their Businesses," http://business.time.com/tag/top-10-companies-that-changed-their-core-products/

2. "National Cash Register Company," http://www.ohiohistorycentral.org/w/National_Cash_Register_Company

3. "How to Reinvent Your Brand," http://adage.com/artil/cmo-strategy/reinvent-brand/3057543

4. "Can a Company Live Forever?," http://www.bbc.com/news/business-16611040

5. "Old Spice Case Study: How a 75-year-old Brand Changed Digital Marketing Forever," http://www.digitaltrainingacademy.com/casestudies/2011/06/old_spice_case_study_how_a_75yearold_brand_changed_digital_marketing_forever.php

6. "Top Corporate Mergers: The Good, the Bad & the Ugly," http://www.rasmussen.edu/degrees/business/blog/best-and-worst-corporate-mergers/

7. "Burberry's CEO on Turning an Aging British Icon into a Global Luxury Brand," https://hbr.org/2013/01/burberrys-ceo-on-turning-an-aging-british-icon-into-a-global-luxury-brand

8. "How Lego Came Back from the Brink of Bankruptcy," http://www.businessinsider.com/how-lego-made-a-huge-turnaround-2014-2

9. "How P&G's Marc Pritchard Plans to Consolidate Agencies," http://adage.com/article/agency-news/p-g-s-marc-pritchard-plans-consolidate-agencies/298225/

10. "Case Study: The Digital Transformation of McGraw-Hill's Textbook Business," https://salesbenchmarkindex.com/insights/case-study-the-digital-transformation-of-mcgraw-hills-textbook-business/

11. "Actually, People Love Change," http://timkastelle.org/blog/2012/11/actually-people-love-change/

Chapter 3

1. "Should Marketing Be a Linear Process?," https://www.ama.org/publications/MarketingNews/Pages/should-marketing-linear-process.aspx

2. "Preparing Your Board to Navigate Disruption? Marketers Can Help," https://www.forbes.com/sites/kimberlywhitler/2017/02/19/preparing-your-board-to-navigate-disruption-marketers-can-help/#47a24c974ef9

3. "Focus Groups Fall out of Favor," https://www.wsj.com/articles/focus-groups-fall-out-of-favor-1474250702

4. "Five Focus Groups That Saved the World," https://www.research-live.com/article/features/five-focus-groups-that-changed-the-world/id/5018642

5. "Clorox's CMO: 'We are too slow, and we are trying very hard to move faster,'" https://digiday.com/marketing/cloroxs-cmo-slow-trying-hard-move-faster/

6. "Elon Musk Takes Customer Complaint on Twitter from Idea to Execution in 6 Days," http://www.inc.com/justin-bariso/elon-musk-takes-customer-complaint-on-twitter-from-idea-to-execution-in-6-days.html

7. "Examples of Online Communities," https://www.lynda.com/Facebook-tutorials/Examples-online-communities/429631/452879-4.html#tab

8. "Six Successful Examples of Online Brand Communities," https://econsultancy.com/blog/68720-six-successful-examples-of-online-brand-communities/

9. "Stories That Deliver Business Insights," http://sloanreview.mit.edu/article/stories-that-deliver-business-insights/

10. "Building Customer Insights in the Data and Digital Age," http://www.cmo.com.au/article/606904/building-customer-insights-data-digital-age/

11. "Your Frontline Employees Hold the Key to Improving Your Customer Experience," https://www.forbes.com/sites/adrianswinscoe/2017/03/23/your-frontline-employees-hold-the-keys-to-improving-your-customer-experience/#2b8cb9fd50e6

12. "Offline and Marketing Events Remain a Key Strategy for Communication with Clients and Prospects," http://www.thedrum.com/news/2017/07/27/offline-and-marketing-events-remain-key-strategy-communication-with-clients-and

13. "A Guide to Smarter Marketing in Today's Consumer-centric Ecosystem," https://www.forbes.com/sites/strategyand/2016/12/01/a-guide-to-smarter-marketing-in-todays-consumer-centric-ecosystem/#560d4ee71d66

14. "How Intuit Reinvents Itself," http://fortune.com/2017/10/20/how-intuit-reinvents-itself/

15. "SHRM 2015 Employee Recognition Report," http://go.globoforce.com/rs/862-JIQ-698/images/Globoforce_SHRM_2015.pdf

16. "Employee Engagement & Loyalty Statistics: The Ultimate Collection," http://blog.accessperks.com/employee-engagement-loyalty-statistics-the-ultimate-collection

17. "Why John Deere Measures Employee Morale Every Two Weeks," https://hbr.org/2016/05/why-john-deere-measures-employee-morale-every-two-weeks

18. "MarTech and the Decade of the CMO," https://foundationcapital.com/wp-content/uploads/2016/08/DotCMO_whitepaper.pdf

19. "Single Customer View Is a 20-Year-Old Idea—So Why Aren't We There Yet?," http://www.mycustomer.com/marketing/data/

single-customer-view-is-a-20-year-old-idea-so-why-arent-we-
there-yet

20. "A Different Way to Achieve a Single View of the Customer,"
    https://www.forbes.com/sites/adrianswinscoe/2015/09/09/a-
    different-way-to-achieve-a-single-view-of-the-customer/
    #1d740c0f687b

21. "The 2015 Customer Experience ROI Study," http://www.water-
    markconsult.net/docs/Watermark-Customer-Experience-ROI-
    Study.pdf

22. "The Customer Is Wrong and Cannot Be Trusted," http://
    www.business2community.com/customer-experience/customer-
    wrong-cannot-trusted-01381171#3gMWRTpjZdwhpD7a.97

23. "4 Reasons CMOs Are Top Candidates for CEO Succession,"
    https://www.ama.org/publications/MarketingNews/Pages/
    customer-driven-b2b-cmos-become-ceos.aspx

Chapter 4

1. "ScrumAlliance 30-Second Video Overview," https://www.
   scrumalliance.org/why-scrum

2. "What Are the 9 Types of Agility in the Agility Series?," https://
   www.linkedin.com/pulse/what-9-types-agility-series-larry-cooper

3. "Putting Agility into How You Do Business," https://www.apqc.
   org/blog/putting-agility-how-you-do-business

4. "10 Workplace Trends You'll See in 2017," https://www.forbes.
   com/sites/danschawbel/2016/11/01/workplace-trends-2017/
   #5856b9e956bd

5. "National Research Council Canada," http://www.nrc-cnrc.gc.
   ca/eng/

6. "We've Selected You for a Special Assignment—Congratulations!?,"
   https://www.linkedin.com/pulse/20141003003003-101139834-
   we-ve-selected-you-for-a-special-assignment-congratulations

7. "Microsoft: CMOs Are Not Comfortable with the Growing Role of Tech," https://www.marketingweek.com/2017/03/28/microsoft-technology-cmos/

8. "Korn Ferry Survey," http://www.marketwatch.com/story/korn-ferry-survey-87-percent-of-executives-want-to-be-ceo-yet-only-15-percent-of-execs-are-learning-agile-a-key-to-effective-leadership-2014-10-02

9. "Can AT&T Retrain 100,000 People?," http://fortune.com/att-hr-retrain-employees-jobs-best-companies/

10. "Equipping People to Stay Ahead of Technological Change," http://www.economist.com/news/leaders/21714341-it-easy-say-people-need-keep-learning-throughout-their-careers-practicalities

11. "Introducing RBC Future Launch," http://www.rbc.com/newsroom/news/2017/20170328-rbc-future_cnews.html

12. "How to Get Trained by Facebook's CMO for a Job in Social Media," http://www.cnbc.com/2017/01/17/how-to-get-trained-by-facebooks-cmo-for-a-job-in-social-media.html

13. "Survey Reveals the Companies That Develop the Best C-level Marketing Leaders," https://www.forbes.com/sites/kimberlywhitler/2016/08/21/best-companies-for-developing-c-level-marketing-leaders/#2ca26e444c31

Chapter 5

1. "Mark Ritson: Marketing Debate Is So Polarized It's Hard to Be Sure of Anything," https://www.marketingweek.com/2017/08/02/mark-ritson-polarised-marketing-debate/

2. "Average Tenure of CMO Continues to Decline," https://www.wsj.com/articles/average-tenure-of-cmo-continues-to-decline-1489777765

3. "Preparing Your Board to Navigate Disruption? Marketers Can Help," https://www.forbes.com/sites/kimberlywhitler/2017/02/19/preparing-your-board-to-navigate-disruption-marketers-can-help/#640cdb074ef9

4. "CMOs First on Firing Line When Companies Miss Growth Goals," http://adage.com/article/cmo-strategy/cmos-fired-companies-miss-goals/306561/

5. "The Crisis of Meaningfulness in Marketing," http://www.campaignlive.com/article/crisis-meaningfulness-marketing/1414636

6. "The FTC Isn't Going to Save Influencer Marketing from Itself, but the Industry Could," http://marketingland.com/ftc-isnt-going-save-influencer-marketing-industry-196129

7. "The Trouble with CMOs," https://hbr.org/2017/07/the-trouble-with-cmos

8. "National Center for Education Statistics (NCES)," https://nces.ed.gov/programs/coe/indicator_cta.asp

9. "Bureau of Labor Statistics, Occupational Outlook Handbook, 2014-2024," https://www.bls.gov/ooh/management/advertising-promotions-and-marketing-managers.htm#tab-6

10. "The CMO Personality Vs. the C-suite Personality [Study]," https://talentculture.com/the-cmo-personality-vs-the-c-suite-personality-study/

11. "Agility Is Not the Answer," https://www.cebglobal.com/blogs/want-more-performance-from-your-employees-agility-is-not-the-answer/

12. "Leading Effectively When You Inherit a Mess," https://hbr.org/2017/08/leading-effectively-when-you-inherit-a-mess

Chapter 6

1. "You Now Have a Shorter Attention Span Than a Goldfish," http://time.com/3858309/attention-spans-goldfish/

2. "The Case for Creativity," http://www.thecaseforcreativity.com/#home

3. "The Creative Dividend: How Creativity Impacts Business Results," https://landing.adobe.com/dam/downloads/whitepapers/55563.en.creative-dividends.pdf

4. "Creativity in Advertising: When It Works and When It Doesn't," https://hbr.org/2013/06/creativity-in-advertising-when-it-works-and-when-it-doesnt

5. "Whoa: Marketing Technology Budgets Are Now Surpassing Advertising," http://chiefmartec.com/2016/05/marketing-technology-budgets-surpassed-advertising/

6. "Tell Your Kids to Be Data Scientists, Not Doctors," https://www.wired.com/insights/2014/06/tell-kids-data-scientists-doctors/

7. "2016-2017 Gartner CMO Spend Survey Reveals the CMO's Growing Mandate," http://www.gartner.com/smarterwithgartner/2016-2017-gartner-cmo-spend-survey-reveals-the-cmos-growing-mandate/

8. "Data Scientist: The Sexiest Job of the 21st Century," https://hbr.org/2012/10/data-scientist-the-sexiest-job-of-the-21st-century

9. "Marketing Technology Landscape Supergraphic (2017): Martech 5000," http://chiefmartec.com/2017/05/marketing-techniology-landscape-supergraphic-2017/

10. "Live Video Has Become the Creative Canvas for Digital Marketers," https://marketingland.com/live-video-become-creative-canvas-digital-marketers-210983

11. "People: The Achilles' Heel of Online Marketers," http://marketingland.com/people-achilles-heel-online-marketers-211987

12. "Six Jobs Are Eliminated for Every Robot Introduced into the Workforce, a New Study Says," https://www.recode.net/2017/3/28/15094424/jobs-eliminated-new-robots-workforce-industrial

13. "Weber Shandwick Press Release," https://www.webershandwick.com/news/article/global-consumers-are-seven-times-more-likely-to-see-a-positive-than-negativ

14. "Walt Disney and the Imagineers," http://www.insidethemagic.net/2011/03/interview-answering-how-do-i-become-an-imagineer-with-disney-artist-don-carson/

15. "Burger King CMO Says Brands Must Respect Agencies as Partners, Not Dismiss Them as Vendors," http://www.adweek.com/agencies/

burger-king-cmo-says-brands-must-respect-agencies-as-partners-not-dismiss-them-as-vendors/

16. "What Marketers Can Learn from Thomas Friedman's Advice for the Rest of Us," https://www.act-on.com/blog/what-marketers-can-learn-from-thomas-friedmans-advice-for-the-rest-of-us/

17. "9 Ways to Become More Creative in the Next 10 Minutes," https://www.inc.com/larry-kim/9-ways-to-become-more-creative-in-the-next-10-minutes.html

18. "Bored with Brainstorming? Try These Five Creativity Boosters," https://www.marketingprofs.com/articles/2017/32231/bored-with-brainstorming-try-these-five-creativity-boosters?adref=nlt060717

Chapter 7

1. "Let Your Workers Rebel," https://hbr.org/cover-story/2016/10/let-your-workers-rebel

2. "The Troubling Rise of 'Me-dership,'" https://www.kornferry.com/institute/me-first-leadership

3. "Millennials: The Me, Me, Me Generation," http://time.com/247/millennials-the-me-me-me-generation/

4. "Bureau of Labor Statistics News Release," https://www.bls.gov/news.release/pdf/nlsoy.pdf

5. "Netflix Case Study," https://www.slideshare.net/JulienGuitton/netflix-case-study-54240175

6. "Netflix Quarterly Earnings, Q3, 2018," https://ir.netflix.com/results.cfm

7. "Tesla Generates Small Sales, Big Buzz, Without Paid Ads," http://adage.com/article/news/tesla-generates-small-sales-big-buzz-paid-ads/241994/

8. "Tesla's Marketing Strategy: Don't Just Make Electric Cars, Sell a Slice of the Future," https://www.referralcandy.com/blog/tesla/

9. "3 Inbound Marketing Best Practices to Steal for 2017," https://www.entrepreneur.com/article/287171#

10. "Partnering for Performance: Part 4: The CFO and the Chief Marketing Officer," http://www.ey.com/Publication/vwLUAssets/EY-partnering-for-performance-the-cfo-and-the-chief-marketing-officer/$FILE/ey-partnering-for-performance-the-cfo-and-cmo.pdf

11. "The 70:20:10 Model for Learning and Development," https://www.trainingindustry.com/wiki/the-702010-model-for-learning-and-development/

12. "A Taste of 70/20/10 Content from Coca-Cola," http://www.abzcreativepartners.com/taste-702010-content-coca-cola-2/

Chapter 8

1. How to Find the Right Marketing Leader for Your Company," http://www.cmswire.com/digital-marketing/how-to-find-the-right-marketing-leader-for-your-company/

2. "Unilever Consolidates Local and Global Marketing Units," https://www.campaignlive.com/article/unilever-consolidates-local-global-marketing-units/1409760

3. "The Reasons Behind Unilever's Marketing Cuts," https://www.marketingweek.com/2017/04/13/reasons-unilever-marketing-cuts/

4. "Businesses with Brilliant Global Marketing Strategies," https://blog.hubspot.com/marketing/global-marketing-and-international-business

5. "Steven Overman Hopes It's Time for Another Kodak Moment," http://www.cmo.com/interviews/articles/2016/9/23/the-cmocom-interview-steven-overman-cmo-kodak.html#gs.6pGg=nM

6. "Gallup: Employee Engagement in U.S. Stagnant in 2015," http://www.gallup.com/poll/188144/employee-engagement-stagnant-2015.aspx

7. "No ... People Are NOT Our Greatest Asset," https://www.linkedin.com/pulse/20140604055030-45973987-no-people-

are-not-our-greatest-asset?articleId=5879831202382254080#
comments-5879831202382254080&trk=prof-post

8. "Studies Show Marketers Missing the Mark—Transformation
and Skills Development Required," https://www.forbes.com/
sites/johnellett/2014/10/31/studies-show-marketers-missing-the-
mark-transformation-and-skills-development-required/#-
72572da1c20b

9. "Oracle Study Demonstrates Business Impact of Modern Marketing
Best Practices," http://www.oracle.com/us/corporate/press/2332354

10. "Outsider CEOs Are on the Rise at the World's Biggest
Companies," https://hbr.org/2016/04/outsider-ceos-are-on-the-
rise-at-the-worlds-biggest-companies

11. "Most Reorgs Aren't Ambitious Enough," https://hbr.org/2017/02/
most-reorgs-arent-ambitious-enough

12. "Chief Marketing Officer Optimism at Four-Year High, Proving
the Value of Marketing Remains Elusive," https://cmosurvey.
org/2013/08/chief-marketing-officer-optimism-at-four-year-
high-proving-the-value-of-marketing-remains-elusive/

13. "7 Signs It's Time to Outsource Your Marketing," https://www.
forbes.com/sites/jaysondemers/2014/10/14/7-signs-its-time-to-
outsource-your-marketing/#c7cb1dfc53a5

14. "US Bureau of Labor Statistics: Employer Costs for Employee
Compensation," https://www.bls.gov/news.release/ecec.nr0.htm

15. "Sony Computer Entertainment America to Provide Consumer
Refunds to Settle FTC Changes over Misleading Ads for
PlayStation Vita Gaming Console," https://www.ftc.gov/news-
events/press-releases/2014/11/sony-computer-entertainment-
america-provide-consumer-refunds

Chapter 9

1. "Oreo's Super Bowl Power-Outage Tweet Was 18 Months in
the Making," http://www.businessinsider.com/oreos-super-
bowl-power-outage-tweet-was-18-months-in-the-making-2013-3

2. "Percent of a Business Budget for Salary," http://smallbusiness.chron.com/percent-business-budget-salary-14254.html

3. "New Study Finds Freelance Economy Grew to 55 million Americans This Year, 35 Percent of Total U.S. Workforce," http://www.marketwired.com/press-release/new-study-finds-freelance-economy-grew-55-million-americans-this-year-35-total-us-workforce-2164446.htm

4. "7½ Reasons to Hire a Fractional CMO," https://www.serebrinpartners.com/single-post/2016/08/27/7-%C2%BD-Reasons-to-Hire-a-Fractional-CMO

5. "What Does a Fractional CMO Cost?," https://www.chiefoutsiders.com/blog/fractional-cmo-cost

6. "2017 Deloitte Global Human Capital Trends," https://www2.deloitte.com/us/en/pages/human-capital/articles/introduction-human-capital-trends.html

7. "Disruption in the C-suite," https://www.entrepreneur.com/article/282060

8. "McDonald's Ends 41-year Olympic Sponsorship As Part of Its 'New Global Growth Plan,'" https://www.marketingweek.com/2017/06/16/mcdonalds-olympics-sponsorship/

9. "A Guide to Smarter Marketing in Today's Consumer-centric Ecosystem," https://www.forbes.com/sites/strategyand/2016/12/01/a-guide-to-smarter-marketing-in-todays-consumer-centric-ecosystem/#5a0e9d911d66

10. "Why Unilever Is Halving Its Agencies and Investing in Strategy," http://adage.com/article/cmo-strategy/weed-root-waste-agencies-unilever-alike/309631/

11. "How P&G's Marc Pritchard Plans to Consolidate Agencies," http://adage.com/article/agency-news/p-g-s-marc-pritchard-plans-consolidate-agencies/298225/

12. "P&G Cuts Agencies 40 Percent in First Wave of Consolidation Drive," http://adage.com/article/ad-age-research/p-g-cuts-agencies-40-wave-consolidation/299750/

13. "P&G to Cut Agency Roster by Another 50 Percent As It Looks to 'Reinvent' Relationships," https://www.marketingweek. com/2018/01/23/pg-cut-agency-roster-another-50-looks-reinvent-relationships/

14. "Global Consultancies Are Buying up Agencies and Reshaping the Brand Marketing World," http://www.adweek.com/ brand-marketing/global-consultancies-are-buying-up-agencies-and-reshaping-the-brand-marketing-world/

15. "The CMO Survey: Highlights and Insights," https://cmosurvey. org/results/february-2017/

Chapter 10

1. "Marketing Technology Landscape Supergraphic (2017): Martech 5000," http://chiefmartec.com/2017/05/marketing-techniology-landscape-supergraphic-2017/

2. "Companies with a Formal Sales Process Generate More Revenue," https://hbr.org/2015/01/companies-with-a-formal-sales-process-generate-more-revenue

3. "Do You Speak the Language of Business?," https://executive education.wharton.upenn.edu/thought-leadership/wharton-at-work/2013/07/language-of-business

4. "Humans Process Visual Data Better," http://www.t-sciences.com/ news/humans-process-visual-data-better

5. "3 Ways Data Dashboard Can Mislead You," https://hbr.org/ 2017/01/3-ways-data-dashboards-can-mislead-you

6. "Five Management Tips to Improve Project Results," https://www. bizjournals.com/bizjournals/how-to/growth-strategies/2017/05/ five-management-tips-to-improve-project-results.html

7. "Five Things You May Not Have Known About PMOs," https:// www.planacademy.com/5-things-you-may-not-have-known-about-pmo/

Chapter 11

1. "How Long Does It Actually Take to Form a New Habit? (Backed by Science)," http://jamesclear.com/new-habit

2. "18 Facts About Goals and Their Achievement," http://www.goalband.co.uk/goal-achievement-facts.html

3. "Wikipedia: CliffsNotes," https://en.wikipedia.org/wiki/CliffsNotes

Conclusion

1. "CMOs First on Firing Line When Companies Miss Growth Goals," http://adage.com/article/cmo-strategy/cmos-fired-companies-miss-goals/306561/

2. "15 of the Best Marketers of Our Time," http://blog.cloudpeeps.com/15-best-marketers/

ABOUT THE AUTHOR

As a former VP of marketing and VP of sustainability for Fortune global companies, **Engelina Jaspers** knows that delivering tangible business results is crucial—not only to the success of your organization, but to the success and longevity of your career too.

Over the past thirty years, she has worked for some of the finest consumer and technology brands. She's been privileged to partner with smart business leaders in building high-performing teams and turbocharging their marketing investments and sustainability credentials.

Along the way, Engelina led a number of complex business transformations requiring diplomacy, diligence, and change leadership. These experiences led her to develop the *Marketing Flexology* management framework—a mindset and a toolset for outsmarting change and future-proofing your career, your team, and your marketing platform.

As VP of corporate marketing and global citizenship for Flex, Engelina led a pivotal transformation of the Flex strategy, corporate identity, and brand internally across 100 global sites and 200,000 employees and externally through storytelling tools, high-profile events, and visual identity assets. She and her team also crafted a new global citizenship strategy, direction, set of key initiatives, and external website that aligned their company's strategy with the UN's Sustainable Development goals.

As VP of marketing strategy and effectiveness for HP, Engelina led a global PMO and ten work streams that aligned her company under a focused global strategy and set of marketing priorities . . . and delivered $172M in savings within six months.

When Greenpeace appeared on the rooftop, she was tapped to drive a turnaround for her company's sustainability efforts and named VP of environmental sustainability for HP. Two years later, HP was ranked #1 greenest consumer electronics company by Greenpeace, #5 best global green brand by Interbrand, and #2 on *Newsweek's* Global 100 Greenest Companies ratings.

Engelina now shares what she's learned through customized workshops, presentations, and collaborations, where she provides real-world insights, practical tools, and actionable steps to help you "up your game," grow your mindshare and market share, and stay ahead of your company's ever-changing business dynamics. Find out more at www.marketingflexology.com and connect with her on Twitter @Ready2Flex.

ONE LAST CTA

Most leaders can solve their own problems. But sometimes, a little extra push is needed to coax reluctant team members, or to kickstart a change initiative. Bringing in an unbiased, experienced, outside perspective oftentimes can make all the difference. I am available for:

- Individual and group collaborations
- Half- and full-day workshops
- Employee training programs
- Customized speaking engagements

As an added incentive, special book discounts are available on quantity purchases by corporations, associations, universities, and others. Don't waste another good crisis by being unprepared. Contact engelina@marketingflexology.com now.

www.ingramcontent.com/pod-product-compliance
Lightning Source LLC
Chambersburg PA
CBHW021053210326
41598CB00016B/1198